Contents

Introduction

Think of the last time you overpacked a suitcase for a trip. Many presenters do the same with their presentations, trying to include everything they know. In a micro presentation (5-10 minutes), you can only include the essentials. We cover core message identification, structure, audience engagement, scripting, pacing, and confidence building for short presentations. Developing micro presentations is a valuable skill despite its challenges.

In various organizational roles today, working with data is essential. Whether it is a simple survey or a complex data analysis project, both experienced professionals and newcomers often feel the need to enhance their data-related skills. As we are exposed to better data storytelling in journalism, TED Talks, and other sources, the expectations for data presentations have risen. We will learn strategic mindset shift, best practices, and practical tips to enhance your data-driven presentations. The goal is to help you inform and inspire your audiences, making a more significant impact within your organization or relevant field. Topics covered include data literacy, communication strategies, organizing ideas, storytelling, visualization, and presentation skills.

An age-old saying suggests, "Storytellers wield great influence." You will learn the art of compelling storytelling for both personal and business connections. You will enhance your storytelling, writing, and presentation abilities, empowering you to become a formidable storyteller.

When you give a compelling presentation, your end result is a message that leaves your audience informed, fulfilled, and often inspired to take action. To be an effective speaker, you must deeply understand your audience, including their motivations, whether it is success, recognition, or profit. You learn how to creating a business presentation from idea generation to delivery, covering audience analysis, message design, visuals, and essential presentation skills. Before your presentation, gather feedback on the topic, assess past discussions, and understand any dissenting opinions to better prepare.

To achieve success in science, you must effectively communicate with your stakeholders, leading to positive outcomes like collaboration, funding, recognition, and idea adoption. I will share innovative strategies to revolutionize your technical presentations, ensuring you never present your science the same way again. Successful science communicators exhibit three key qualities: a compelling science narrative, genuine passion, and a deep understanding of their audience's needs. Bridging the gap between your technical work and stakeholders is the ultimate goal.

Your audience forms a quick opinion about you within seconds, so it is crucial to establish credibility immediately. We will focus on gaining credibility within the first 30 seconds of your speech or presentation. We will begin learning how to create a strong initial impression.

Imagine being asked to present to your company's senior executives, the C-suite. This is a great opportunity to enhance your professional standing. You will learn how to prepare, present, and follow up effectively. You will gain insights into handling challenging situations. We will equip you with the essential tools to advance your career through exposure to senior executives.

In our busy lives, scheduling face-to-face meetings can be challenging. Fortunately, modern technology allows us to conduct effective meetings through video, whether on our computers or phones. While starting a video call may seem straightforward, there are strategic approaches to make your video presentations impactful. We will help you prepare for video meetings and showcase your professionalism.

Effective communication is crucial in both professional and personal contexts. However, many of us experience anxiety when speaking in front of others. We will learn actionable strategies to manage anxiety symptoms and sources, while eliminating counterproductive behaviors. Everyone has valuable stories, insights, and ideas to share, but learning to control anxiety empowers us to confidently engage in meaningful conversations.

Chapter 1 Micro-Presentations: Saying More in Less Time

Examples of micro-presentations

The Academy Awards for the acceptance speeches, which are essentially micro presentations lasting 45 seconds. In today's world, there's a growing need for concise presentations due to short attention spans and online meetings. Just like fun size candy bars, these micro presentations offer the same impact in a smaller package. Opportunities for them exist in the workplace, industry events, and volunteer work. You might need to present updates, project reports, or introductions in various settings. So, consider where micro presentations could fit into your upcoming speaking engagements.

Identifying your audience

Have you ever experienced a workshop where the presenter's content either went over your head or was too basic? Both scenarios result from presenters not understanding their audience. It is crucial to research your audience before crafting your presentation. Knowing their objectives, expectations, background, and industry experience is vital for engaging them effectively. You can conduct audience research in three main ways:

1. Talk to the event organizer, as they have valuable insights about the attendees.

2. Send a survey to the attendees to learn about their backgrounds and expectations.

3. Connect with attendees before and during the presentation, whether through email, conversations, or early arrival, to gather last-minute insights and tailor your content accordingly. The more you tailor your presentation to your audience, the more value you provide. Gathering audience information can significantly improve your presentation's impact.

Recognizing your objective

Have you ever faced the challenge of condensing years of expertise into a short presentation? While this can be overwhelming, time constraints can actually help you focus on what truly matters. To do this effectively, you need a clear objective, which combines your presentation goal with your audience's expectations. Ask yourself two key questions: What specific outcomes do you want from your presentation, such as behavior change, skill acquisition, or a call to action? And, what results are your audience seeking, like inspiration or problem-solving? By aligning your goals with your audience's needs, you can create a presentation that satisfies both, ensuring a successful outcome. Your objective guides your content, core points, and call to action, making your presentation effective and fulfilling for all.

Core message

One of the most memorable commercials, the Old Spice "Man Your Man Could Smell Like," conveys a single message in just 30 seconds: Buy this body wash for your man, and he transforms into the perfect partner. Commercials, like micro presentations, should focus on one core message. To determine your core message, analyze your topic, consider your audience's needs, and identify what you both want to achieve. Then, narrow down and refine your concept to be clear and concise. In a micro presentation, brevity is key to ensuring your audience understands your message. Start exploring your topics and refining them into a clear, relevant core message for your next presentation.

Call to action

If you want to see a master of micro presentations in action, watch a home shopping channel. These hosts excel at delivering a persuasive call to action. In every presentation, whether you are informing, proposing, or sharing, you are essentially selling an idea or action to your audience. Just like home shopping hosts prompt viewers to buy, you must clearly instruct your audience on what to do after your presentation. This is your call to action, and it's essential for micro presentations. Determine the action you want your audience to take, whether it is contacting you, supporting a cause, or making a purchase. Without a clear call to action, your audience may not know how to proceed, potentially missing out on valuable opportunities. So, review your presentations and ensure you provide explicit instructions for the desired next steps to make a significant impact.

Structure

Have you ever paid attention to the structure of a movie? Even though it may not be obvious, every movie, just like every presentation, follows a structured journey. Presentations, including micro presentations, consist of three key parts: the opening, the body, and the closing. The opening captures the audience's interest, while the body delivers the core content, typically with no more than three main points in a micro presentation. Finally, the closing and call to action wrap up the ideas and instruct the audience on their next steps. A clear and concise structure is vital in micro presentations to prevent confusion and ensure a smooth audience journey towards your objective. It is crucial to stay organized and stick to the structure in short presentations, so your message is well-defined and your audience remains engaged.

Opening

In presentations, starting with credentials or thank-you is a no-go; micro presentations require engaging openings. The beginning is a crucial moment to grab your audience's attention, so make them laugh, arouse curiosity, or shock them with an intriguing comment, story, or statistic. Humor, questions, or short quizzes with rewards can also captivate your audience initially. Your goal is to pique their interest, ensuring they stay focused for the next few minutes. Avoid the rookie mistake of neglecting an engaging opening in your micro presentation.

Core points

Ever been lost in a big store, craving direction to find butter? Life and presentations can feel bewildering without clear navigation. In a micro presentation, structure is vital for the audience's journey.

Start with your core message and concept, and outline your core points. Here are four effective structures:

1. Chronological: Present a timeline, past to future, explaining the "why, what, where, how, and who."

2. Global to Local: Describe the topic from a broad perspective to a detailed one, showing differences.

3. Sandwich: Share a positive, negative, and another positive, providing balance and a way forward.

4. List: Deliver a set of points, like "top five ways" or "five tips," to highlight reasons or improvements.

These structures offer different ways to convey the same message. A clear structure makes designing concise micro presentations easier, ensuring your audience follows the path you lead them on. Which structure do you use or plan to try in your presentations? Do not leave your audience wandering; guide them like finding butter.

Closing

Leaving a party can be challenging, much like ending a presentation. Many speakers struggle with knowing when and how to conclude. It is a bit like what Henry Wadsworth Longfellow said: "Great is the art of beginning, but greater the art is of ending."

Here are some compelling reasons to put thought into your closing:

1. Clarity: The audience needs to know when you are done. Ambiguity is awkward. Always signal the end, even if it is just by saying thank you.

2. Reinforcement: Your closing is an opportunity to reinforce your core message, especially if you have covered several points during your presentation.

3. Call to Action: You can challenge the audience to take action. What do you want them to do as a result of your presentation? Make your call to action clear.

4. Memorability: This is your chance to leave a lasting impression. Share something interesting, funny, profound, or thought-provoking. You can use powerful images, quotes, or wrap up a story started at the beginning.

A strong closing brings your presentation full circle and ensures your big idea sticks with the audience, wrapping it up effectively.

Timing

In a micro-presentation, timing is the most critical factor. With a limited slot of 5 or 10 minutes, you cannot go off-topic or waste time. Break your presentation into segments and determine the time for each. For a 5-minute presentation, allocate around 1 minute for the opening and 30 seconds for the closing, leaving 1 minute and 10 seconds for each of the three core points.

Consider these timing tips:

1. Prepare and Time Each Segment Separately: Ensure you can deliver each point within its allocated time, estimating about 130 words per minute.

2. Build in a Time Cushion: Plan for your presentation to be slightly shorter than the allocated time to account for interruptions, errors, and late starts.

3. Practice Out Loud: You cannot rehearse this in your head. Practice your opening, core points, and closing, trimming any excess content. This ensures your micro-presentation hits the mark in terms of timing.

Purpose of engagement

To make your audience learn and remember what you teach, remember three key things about engagement:

1. Emotional Activation: Engagement evokes emotions in your audience.

2. Relevance and Interest: Emotional connection makes your content more relevant and interesting.

3. Retention and Learning: When content is relevant and interesting, your audience pays attention and retains more information.

Acknowledging emotions is essential because they influence behavior and attitudes. Your audience experiences emotions during your presentation, and so do you. You can leverage these emotions to connect with your audience effectively.

Ask yourself:

- What's funny about my topic?

- What's frustrating?

- What's inspiring?

- What stirs anger, curiosity, or desperation?

For instance, consider what amuses or irritates you and your colleagues at work, what inspires you, or what causes frustration. Integrate these emotional aspects into your presentation with stories, activities, and examples. By activating emotions around your topic, your presentation becomes more engaging, memorable, meaningful, and effective in creating change.

Engagement tools

In micro presentations, engagement tools are crucial to maintain audience interest. Here are a few effective tools:

1. Stories: Stories, whether analogies, examples, fables, or case studies, resonate with humans who are naturally wired to learn from them. Keep stories concise to illustrate your core message or main points effectively.

2. Group Discussions and Online Chats: Encourage your audience to share their thoughts, feelings, and experiences through discussions, whether in person or in virtual environments.

3. Worksheets and Handouts: Provide worksheets before your presentation and ask the audience to complete them as you go through your content.

4. Quick Polls and Questionnaires: Use polls, questionnaires, and quizzes to gather information and feedback. With careful planning, these can fit into a micro presentation.

Engagement tools not only enhance learning but also make your concepts memorable. Incorporating these tools into your presentations, regardless of their length, ensures that your message remains meaningful and unforgettable.

To script or not to script

To script or not to script, that's the question when it comes to preparing your micro presentation. Unlike longer presentations, micro-ones require precise timing and structure. You have three options:

1. Script it all: Script your entire content word for word. Pros: Precise timing. Cons: Need to sound conversational, and not everyone is good at reading or memorizing scripts.

2. Script the opening, closing, and core points: Pros: Strong structure with room for flexibility. Cons: Risk of going off on tangents or wasting time.

3. Script only bullet points: Useful for quick preparations but mainly has cons. Effective if you're knowledgeable about the topic, can speak concisely, and stay on track.

I encourage you to spend some time scripting your micro presentation to maintain organization and ensure it flows smoothly within the allotted time.

Editing for impact

Editing is essential when crafting a micro presentation. Do not edit as you go; complete a full draft first. Record yourself practicing and note timing, long sentences, breath pauses, and flow. Edit by rearranging and cutting content. Identify and remove the following:

1. The fat: Relevant but excessive content that does not fit.

2. The flat: Dry data and unnecessary details.

3. The fluff: Entertaining but valueless content.

Editing requires letting go of the idea of including all your knowledge to create a concise and impactful presentation.

Pacing

Auctioneers talk quickly to hypnotize bidders, but fast-paced micro presentations come with issues. Speed talking can lead to misunderstanding, especially for non-native speakers or those with hearing impairments, and it can overwhelm the audience.

Slowing down your speech, even if it feels too slow, is essential. It aids audience understanding, allows for better breathing and voice support, and reduces nervousness. Pacing requires practice, so record yourself to monitor clear enunciation, pauses, and breaths. You can almost always speak more slowly to improve your micro presentation.

Overwhelm

During a micro presentation, it is easy to feel overwhelmed, like you are on a fast-paced ride. To handle this feeling:

1. Use a countdown timer for precise time tracking instead of looking at the clock.

2. Do not stress about missed content; it is an opportunity for follow-up resources.

3. Trust yourself to handle any mishaps. Practice and preparation enable on-the-fly adaptation.

Micro presentations can be thrilling and challenging. Trust your preparation to ensure a smooth delivery.

Lack of preparation

In the world of micro-presentations, incomplete preparation can lead to various consequences like losing your place, tech issues, confusion, or running out of time, which can disappoint your audience. Conversely, thorough preparation offers benefits such as audience engagement, learning, and enhanced credibility.

Here are three quick tips for effective preparation:

1. When you accept the speaking engagement, jot down initial thoughts immediately.

2. Make time in your schedule for preparation and practice.

3. Practice your presentation out loud, just as if you were addressing a real audience.

Although preparing a presentation may feel like a task, the rewards for you and your audience are worth the effort.

Conclusion

Crafting micro presentations can be a liberating experience, as the time constraints push you to focus on what truly matters and share your expertise effectively. You can explore the National Speakers Association for valuable resources and networking opportunities.

Chapter 2 Presenting Data Effectively to Inform and Inspire

Develop your data literacy

To effectively present data, you must possess data literacy, which means having the ability to work with data. Your level of data literacy can vary depending on your specific needs and audience. It is not necessary to be a data scientist or a math expert, but your data literacy should match your objectives. For general audiences with a mild interest in summary findings, you do not need deep data expertise. Simple tasks like survey scoring and calculating percentages can suffice.

However, if your audience demands more sophisticated insights or if the data you present has critical implications, you may need a higher level of data literacy and greater precision in your analysis. Your expertise should align with the complexity and importance of your work. Collaborating with experts is also an option to ensure accuracy and precision in your data.

So, understanding your data is the first step in presenting it effectively. Explore how to use your data literacy to uncover interesting and important insights within your data, creating a compelling story for your audience.

Find the "so what" in your data

Ever attended a presentation and wondered, "What is the point?" It is a common experience because many presenters miss what I am about to explain.

This involves data literacy, critical thinking about your data and methodologies, and considering the questions you should ask. However, it is more than just data; it is about finding the real significance.

Use a basic example. Imagine you surveyed people about their ice cream preferences and found that 82 like vanilla, 47 like strawberry, and 16 like pistachio out of 100 respondents. This data may seem mildly interesting, but the "so what" depends on your survey's purpose. If it is about pistachio production, the number 16 is significant. But if you are boosting strawberry sales, the real "so what" might be the discovery that all pistachio lovers also like strawberry.

In essence, the "so what" is not about math; it is about the questions you ask. The question here might be, "What do I know about strawberry ice cream enthusiasts?" which led to the insight about pistachio lovers. Keep in mind that a finding can be interesting but irrelevant. For instance, discovering all pistachio lovers are left-handed is intriguing but unrelated to selling more strawberry ice cream. The "so what" must be pertinent; otherwise, it should be omitted from your presentation.

Three key priorities for data communications

Imagine a dictionary - it has all the words but tells no story. Similarly, a common pitfall in data presentations is providing a list of facts that can feel like reading a dictionary. To transform this, focus is crucial. Eliminate irrelevant information and organize what remains to resonate with your audience. Here are three simple yet terrible acronyms as a mnemonic aid. They are KWYs, which sounds like "why."

The first acronym, KWYRWTS (Know What You Really Want To Say), emphasizes the importance of having a clear perspective on your data. Don't include everything; reflect on your viewpoint and make decisions intentionally.

The second, KWYDIS (Know What Your Data Is Saying), highlights the need for basic data literacy. You don't need to be an expert, but comprehending your data is essential.

The third, KWYANTH (Know What Your Audience Needs To Hear), focuses on understanding your audience's needs rather than their desires or explicit requests. By grasping your audience, your data, and your perspective, you can deliver a truly impactful presentation, which goes far beyond reciting a dictionary.

Make clear predictions and recommendations

After analyzing data and uncovering trends and correlations, the job does not end. You typically analyze data not just for academic curiosity or as a hobby, but to offer guidance for decision-making. There are three primary types of data analysis:

1. Descriptive analytics, which involves understanding what has happened in the past.

2. Predictive analytics, where you make future predictions based on past data.

3. Prescriptive analytics, in which you make recommendations to improve the future.

Predictive and prescriptive analytics build upon descriptive analytics. It is essential to use specific predictive modeling for accurate predictions rather than making vague future claims based solely on the past. For example, if your analysis reveals a link between training opportunities and employee retention, you can predict that an increase in hiring may impact retention. You can then recommend doubling the training budget based on expected hiring rates to achieve specific retention goals. By going beyond descriptive analytics and including predictive and prescriptive analytics, you enhance decision-making with data and provide substantial value to your organization.

Define your audience

Understanding your audience is crucial when delivering a presentation. This involves knowing aspects like their language, age, interests, and knowledge on the topic. Moreover, a single presentation can have multiple audiences with varying interests and priorities. You may have a primary audience, like a Chief Human Resources Officer (CHRO), who will use your data for budget decisions. Other stakeholders, such as a VP, may also be important, while some audience members may have a more peripheral role. To strike the right balance, identify and categorize your audiences, then tailor your presentation to guide each group toward specific actions based on their roles and needs. Avoid overemphasizing less critical audiences, as being inclusive should be balanced with practicality. Consider grouping similar audiences together, even if they have distinct tasks but share common goals. Think critically about your audience's expected actions and align your presentation accordingly.

Forget the data

Individuals who present data fall along a spectrum, ranging from data scientists who are deeply immersed in data to audiences who are uncomfortable with and lack confidence in data-related work. Surprisingly, despite their differing positions on the spectrum, they share a common problem: difficulty presenting data. Data enthusiasts often become so engrossed in data details that they neglect the bigger picture, while audiences are too intimidated by data to provide the essential context. Although the reasons differ, the solution is the same for both groups. When preparing a data presentation, it is crucial to momentarily set aside the data. Data enthusiasts should stop fixating on intricate details, and audiences should cease worrying about them. Instead, concentrate on the narrative and emphasize the actual insights in your data that will help your audience grasp concepts and make informed decisions. It is important to remember that audiences are not interested in your data itself; they care about what the data reveals to guide sound decision-making. So, put the data aside for a moment and concentrate on extracting the essential "so what" that the data can convey.

Tell stories

Describing strawberries as red and juicy or discussing farm smells like hay, dirt, and freshly baked goods makes for a dull collection of facts, much like many data presentations. As a child, I visited a farm, and the air was filled with the scent of freshly cut hay and freshly plowed soil. Upon entering the farm store, I was greeted by the sweet aroma of strawberries. The warmth of the oven-fresh shortcake, combined with vanilla-infused whipped cream, provided a delightful experience. Those strawberries, a brilliant shade of red, released their juices as we savored this perfect mid-June treat in the sun. Now, that is a story, right? It is more than just facts; it is a narrative with a particular order and flow. We instinctively recognize a story because storytelling has been a primary method of passing knowledge for thousands of years. Human evolution has ingrained the need for stories in us.

Research has shown that information presented in a story format is more memorable than a mere collection of related facts. This applies to data storytelling as well; you are more likely to remember the numbers when they are part of a story. Stories also incorporate specific types of words that engage different areas of the brain. The more brain regions activated, the more memorable your story becomes. Using descriptive words like "vanilla-tinged whipped cream" engages the smell center in the brain, a powerful memory and emotion trigger. This principle extends to other senses, such as touch and sight. In data storytelling, you might not always have the vivid material found in stories like strawberry shortcake on a summer farm day. However, aim to move away from presenting mere facts and instead weave your ideas into a narrative. This approach will help your audience connect with and remember your presentation more effectively.

What is a story?

We can simplify the essence of stories into two primary elements: linearity and flow. Linearity is the progression from a starting point to an endpoint, advancing one idea or event incrementally. This concept encapsulates the traditional "beginning, middle, end" structure. But linearity alone does not constitute a story. While ideas follow a linear order, they lack flow, and therefore, do not form a story. Stories require flow, which implies the seamless progression of ideas, concepts, or events, akin to water flowing down a stream. The transitions in a story should feel natural. Flow is crucial, especially in presentations, where bullet points or fragmented thoughts disrupt the audience's understanding. When writing for reading, people can interpret bullet points as shorthand for larger ideas. But speaking in bullet points during a presentation is ineffective. To engage your audience, string sentences together logically using connecting words and phrases to transform individual ideas and facts into a seamless, coherent narrative.

Story frameworks

Storytelling is a powerful tool to help people connect with ideas, but it might not come naturally to everyone. In a professional context, the McKinsey-defined storytelling framework called Situation-Complication-Resolution is highly effective. This framework starts by defining the current state of affairs or context (Situation), introduces a complication or potential conflict (Complication), and concludes with a solution to that complication (Resolution). Many organizations emphasize this format for their stories. However, remember that it's not only for conflicts. You can adapt it to Insights-

Predictions-Recommendations or other story mechanisms. Here are some additional techniques to consider:

1. Make It Human: Use specific examples to illustrate general points. For instance, instead of presenting average dataset numbers, highlight an individual like Divya Patel who embodies those attributes.

2. Chronological Story: Narrate events in chronological order, connecting them smoothly with words like "until finally" to maintain the story's flow, which is especially useful for explaining data changes over time.

3. End with "And": Most data presentations should conclude with a clear next step or direction. Ensure that your presentation provides recommendations, guiding the audience on what to do next based on the information shared.

Feel free to explore various frameworks and techniques, using the ones that suit your narrative and make you comfortable. Connecting with your audience and helping them understand and remember your data is more likely when you tell a story in a way that feels natural to you.

Inject emotion and humanity

Recall the experience of learning to ride a bicycle – the fear, concentration, moments of success, and the emotions that stuck with you over the years. Great stories include emotions, a powerful element that engages the audience and enhances content retention. When possible, evoke emotions in your audience. A study revealed that positive emotions improve the perception, understanding, and memory of data visualizations.

However, it can be challenging to infuse emotions into data presentations, as people may become detached when numbers dominate. To blend data with emotions and humanity, consider personalizing the information with relatable examples. You can also use color strategically, keeping in mind that different colors trigger varied emotional responses (though cultural considerations apply). Incorporating photography and music can make a presentation more emotional and human-centered. Let your own humanity shine through as you present – make eye contact and express emotions. This connection with your audience will enhance their ability to engage with and remember the data. The goal is not manipulation but facilitating accurate data comprehension.

Outline a story

Outlines serve as a thought-organizing framework, ensuring I stay focused and stick to the data's relevant arguments. I draw boxes on a whiteboard and label them, each representing a presentation section, or "bucket." This method maintains structure. This framework guides the narrative, and while you can adjust the outline as needed, it prevents straying into tangential topics. Outlining benefits both content creators and audiences, making presentations more organized, engaging, and easier to follow.

Make your presentation flow logically

You have crafted a great hour-long story for a meeting, but how can you be sure it truly works? Do you need to create the entire presentation and test it for sense and flow? Stories follow a logical sequence, and there is a simple way to ensure your story flows. Imagine having just 60 seconds in an elevator with key audience members. How would you summarize the entire story to them, not just an introduction or teaser, but the full gist? Write out a concise version of the story in complete sentences with connector words, ensuring key ideas connect logically. If a 60-second summary works, it confirms the flow and logic of your story. It may not contain every detail but captures all the vital concepts. Reading it aloud is crucial to spot gaps or awkward transitions. If it feels right, your story is good, and you can proceed with the final presentation. This step is crucial for transforming your data story into an effective educational tool for your audience.

Why make it visual?

When presenting, explaining, and teaching, use visuals extensively, especially when dealing with data. Several reasons support this approach. Approximately 50% of your brain processes visual information, making vision the most vital sense. Humans have a strong preference for visual experiences, demonstrated by the picture superiority effect, wherein people remember information better when presented visually or combined with text. Visual content activates both verbal and visual processing in the brain, improving recall. This effect is more pronounced with age, making visuals more crucial for older audiences. Anscombe's quartet, a statistical phenomenon, highlights the importance of visualizing data. Four seemingly identical datasets reveal their differences only when visualized, emphasizing how visuals unveil patterns, trends, outliers, and insights that are otherwise concealed. Visualizing data is crucial during analysis to reveal insights and during communication to convey these insights to stakeholders effectively. Embrace visual representations of data to leverage how your audience processes information and provide unique insights they would not gain otherwise.

Your audience's pre-attentive brain

When designing visuals for your audience, it is crucial to understand how humans process visual information. One key aspect of visual perception is that it happens pre-attentively, meaning people start making sense of visuals even before consciously focusing on them. This unconscious and instantaneous processing offers an opportunity for effective design decisions.

To optimize visuals for pre-attentive processing, it's essential to leverage strong pre-attentive triggers while minimizing distractions from weaker ones. Research has identified four primary pre-attentive attributes: position on a common scale, contrast, length or area of objects, and tilt or angle. Position helps compare relative positions, contrast highlights differences, length provides a sense of quantity, and tilt or angle helps detect trends.

For example, dot plots are effective because they rely on the perception of relative positions and contrast. Bar charts utilize length, and line charts make use of angles to depict trends. The key is to ensure that the important elements stand out pre-attentively.

Consider your pre-attentive audience when creating visuals, keeping in mind that they will quickly assess your chart. Design with the goal of highlighting specific patterns, trends, or insights while reducing distractions. This approach ensures your audience can grasp the essential information at a glance.

Pick the right visual

Many of us were never taught how to select the right chart for our data, often picking one arbitrarily from our software. However, charts serve distinct purposes and should be chosen with intention. To select the right visual for your data, consider three primary factors.

First, think about what you want your audience to understand or do with your data. Are you focusing on trends over time, the overall distribution, value comparisons, or the part-to-whole relationship within your data? Different needs require different charts.

The Visual Vocabulary, such as the one created by the Financial Times, organizes various chart types based on nine task categories. This tool can guide you in choosing the appropriate chart for your specific task.

Testing your visuals is equally important. Create a chart and show it to someone, asking what they understand, learn, and feel they can do with it. If they are confused or can't perform the intended tasks, consider a different chart.

Above all, choose charts with intention. Remember to start with a clear goal and action you want to enable, and then select visuals strategically, as this will lead to more effective data presentation.

Make the numbers relatable

When dealing with statistics, the worst-case scenario is leaving the audience clueless, and in the best case, they may comprehend whether a number is good or bad. However, truly relatable numbers allow people to grasp their real significance, making them more impactful. The aim of any data presentation should be to provide meaning and insight behind the numbers, not just the numbers themselves. Relatability is especially crucial when discussing complex topics like climate change or when dealing with measures that lack intuitive understanding, such as zettajoules. This concept also holds true when handling very large or very small numbers that are challenging for people to comprehend. For example, Jeff Bezos' wealth is around $200 billion, a staggering figure. To make it relatable, consider that if you stacked his entire fortune in pennies, it would reach the moon and back 40 times. In contrast, the wealth of the average U.S. family would not even breach Earth's atmosphere. Bezos possesses as much wealth as 250,000 American families combined, making it a relatable yet astonishing fact.

Strategic annotations and labeling

In presentations, charts without labels are meaningless, and overly labeled charts are equally confusing. Striking a balance is crucial. Start by labeling the axes to define what they measure and their scale. When presenting data verbally, you can provide context, reducing the need for data point labels. In documents, finding the right labeling balance is challenging. Typically, key data points are labeled to draw attention. Important contextual information can also be labeled, but without overwhelming visuals. Maintain a visual hierarchy, making the most important insights prominent with techniques like bounding boxes, bolder type, and larger fonts. Contextual information should be subtler, and axis labels and fine details should be even more discreet. Balancing labeling and annotation are essential to minimize distractions while maximizing comprehension in every visualization.

Redundancy can be useful

In most data presentations worldwide, you will likely find bar charts, line charts, and pie charts, and there is a good reason for that. Bar charts are excellent for comparing values quickly because humans can easily assess the lengths of bars. However, when dealing with similar data and tasks in a presentation, sticking to a single chart type might be the right choice. For example, if you are showing a series of slides to illustrate different trends over time, using line charts consistently can keep your audience focused on the data itself rather than chart variety. It may seem repetitive, but the key is to make the content interesting, not just the chart types. Additionally, prioritizing data storytelling and editing presentations for the most important content is crucial. You can also consider using a different chart type consistently within a presentation, such as dot plots for comparison charts instead of bar charts throughout. The key is to provide the familiarity your audience needs to focus on the insights without getting distracted by frequent chart changes.

Aesthetics matter in visual experiences

Humans have a natural appreciation for aesthetics, whether it's beautiful faces, art, or landscapes. Aesthetics influence how we perceive and interact with the world, including data visualization. Research from the 1990s showed that we are more forgiving of minor flaws in user interfaces when they are aesthetically pleasing. This principle applies to data visualization as well. Recent studies have demonstrated a strong link between aesthetics and performance in data visualization.

For instance, a study compared various approaches to visualizing the same data and found that the sunburst diagram, despite its circular shape, performed exceptionally well both in terms of data understanding and aesthetic appeal. The more beautiful participants found a visualization, the better it performed.

To create aesthetically pleasing visualizations, apply design best practices. Carefully select colors, make thoughtful typography choices, maintain intentional alignment, avoid clutter, and utilize white space effectively. Creating aesthetically pleasing visuals not only enhances the visual appeal but also helps your audience better understand your data, which should always be the primary goal.

Readable, without being read

If you start a presentation with a text-heavy slide, your audience is likely to tune out and start reading instead of listening. As a presenter, you should aim to engage your audience, provide insights, and answer questions, not just serve as a slide reader. While your slides should be visually engaging, they shouldn't be designed for reading.

It is essential to ensure that the text, numbers, and graphics on your slides are clear and legible. Use high-contrast colors, but avoid drawing excessive attention to labels. Use shorter labels, when possible, to improve readability. Tailor your font and word choices based on the presentation medium, whether it's projected, printed, or displayed on a screen.

Remember that in virtual presentations, like Zoom meetings, it is even easier for your audience to disengage if your slides are not engaging. Make your slides readable, but also make them conducive to listening, and avoid reading them word for word yourself.

The appendix is your friend

As a presenter, my favorite part of every presentation is the appendix, not when I am in the audience but when I am the creator. It is like a junk drawer where I stash all the things I collect along the way—raw data, complex charts, slides colleagues suggest, or my boss's irrelevant ones. This appendix is a place for non-essential but potentially useful content. It is a dumping ground for tangential or supporting material that might come in handy but is not core to the story. It is readily available when needed but does not clutter the main presentation. I love the appendix for being a storage space for rarely used content. You should appreciate and utilize an appendix in your presentations as well.

Ruthless editing

Being a ruthless editor is more important than being a good content creator. After assembling your story and refining it, you might have lost focus in the slide production process. You need to revisit your main message and consider the level of detail necessary for each slide. Remove any unnecessary or confusing elements. Ensure your visuals enhance your arguments, rather than detract from them. Don't cling to irrelevant content due to the sunk cost effect. Be ruthless and eliminate anything that does not improve your presentation. Even at the last moment, you can likely cut 20% and enhance your presentation.

Test your presentation

Humans are prone to numerous cognitive biases, which can impact how we analyze and communicate data. Biases like the curse of knowledge, false consensus effect, confirmation bias, and survivor bias can affect data analysis and presentation. To address these biases, the key is to test your presentation. Share your data with colleagues, mentors, friends, or family members, and ask for their feedback on what they understood, if they got confused, and if your interpretations and recommendations make sense. Use this feedback to improve your presentation and data analysis before presenting to your organization's leadership. It is better to address issues now than later.

Predict questions, prepare answers

Just like trial lawyers, be prepared when making data presentations. Anticipate and have answers ready for common questions about data quality, analysis methodologies, unexpected changes in numbers, or shifts from good to bad. If you cannot predict the answer, ensure you have a plan for how to address it, even if it means admitting that you do not know and directing people to the appropriate sources for answers. Preparedness and agility in presentations are essential for maintaining confidence and credibility with your audience.

Practice, practice, practice

Practice is essential for any presentation, including data-driven ones. It is not just about getting better at pronunciation but also about refining transitions and flow. In a presentation, you must seamlessly transition between topics, and practice helps you do this effectively. To ensure your audience is engaged, emphasize key points and make them feel something when necessary. Great public speakers practice every speech to make it feel natural and engaging, and this advice is equally important for data presentations.

Speak your audience's language

When presenting your well-crafted data-driven story, do not forget about your audience's needs. Tailor your message to resonate with them. Consider your audience's demographics, interests, and sensitivities. For example, in a presentation about older athletes and gender disparities in equestrian events, using the phrase "women of a certain age" with air quotes was a strategic choice to connect with a specific audience (people around 50) who could relate to the cultural implications of the phrase. This audience-focused approach sparked emotions and meaningful discussions, enhancing the impact of the presentation. Always aim to connect with your audience in a way that is uniquely relevant to them for a stronger impact.

Skip the methodology

Your methodology is not the star of your data presentation. While there might be a relentless person in the audience who cares about it, most people don't need, understand, or care about your methodology. Avoid starting your presentation with methodology details. Instead, focus on the "so what," key insights, and recommendations. Be prepared to explain your methodology during Q&A if needed. You can include extensive methodological information in the appendix but do not center your presentation around it.

Say the "so what," not the data points

In your presentation, focus on the meaning, not the data itself. When presenting data, don't just read data points or provide statistical details. Instead, explain the implications of the data. Data presentations are about using data to support or refute an argument, provide evidence, and clarify ideas, not just showcasing raw data.

Say more and less than your slides

When delivering a presentation, the amount you say and what you say depends on your slides. If your slides are simple, you will say more and provide additional context beyond what is on the slide. If the slide is complex, you might say less and focus on the key points, ensuring your audience is not overwhelmed by reading extensive content. The slides are there to support your presentation, guide your narrative, and provide additional information but are not the sole focus. Your presentation is like a lighthouse, not the destination but a guide to keep both you and your audience on the right path.

Talk to your audience, not the screen

During a presentation, avoid turning your back on your audience and merely pointing at your slides. You should make eye contact with your audience, engage with them, and connect on a personal level. Remember that presentations are a form of performance, like reading to children where you use various techniques to make the story come to life. When presenting data, people are not interested in your slides or your design process. They care about the story you are telling, the insights you are providing, and the knowledge you are sharing. Your slides are supporting materials to reinforce your ideas and help you remember the points you want to cover. Instead of reading your slides, focus on interpreting, explaining, and expanding on the information they contain. Exceptionally well-designed slides may attract attention, and if the audience is interested, they can inquire about the design process, but that is not the primary purpose of your presentation.

Bring in live data

Integrate live data into your presentations whenever possible, just like a live musical performance offers a unique experience. While it may seem daunting, the potential benefits often outweigh the risks. Live data allows for spontaneous exploration and can provide deeper insights during your presentation or Q&A. Embrace the opportunity to address nuanced questions on the spot and engage your audience in a more interactive and insightful experience.

Love the data

Genuine belief in your message is the most effective way to connect with your audience. Your passion, enthusiasm, and interest in your data will shine through in your presentation. Even if you do not love the data itself, care about the insights you are providing or be passionate about solving problems. The key is to approach your work with focus, authenticity, and a commitment to finding engaging ways to communicate your data effectively. Embrace the process, develop your skills, and your presentations will consistently improve.

Chapter 3 Storytelling
Introduction to storytelling

A French poet, Jacques Prévert, once encountered a blind beggar and transformed his life by changing his sign from "I'm blind" to "Spring is coming, but I won't see it." This illustrates the profound impact of storytelling, as stories create connections and empathy, making people care. Stories have played a crucial role in various movements, like civil rights, by uniting people from diverse backgrounds. Even experiencing stories together, as in movies, strengthens bonds. Understanding the mechanics of stories empowers you to build relationships, evoke empathy, and bring positive changes to your life and work.

Why great stories build relationships and make people care

Throughout human history, storytelling has played a vital role in our survival, relationship-building, and eliciting empathy. Stories helped early tribes cooperate and remember essential knowledge. Loyalty to countries, families, and organizations often stems from stories that evoke emotions. In business, successful companies are often those that master the art of storytelling, connecting with their audience and building loyalty. Ford and SPAM are examples of companies using stories to enhance their brands. However, it is important to use storytelling for good, as incongruence and dishonesty will eventually be exposed, and authenticity is key for long-term success.

The history of storytelling and why you should care

Stories possess the remarkable ability to immerse us completely, affecting our memory and empathy. When watching a compelling story, our brains and bodies react as if we are part of the narrative, demonstrating empathy and emotional engagement. Unlike mere facts, which engage two brain regions, storytelling activates multiple areas, including emotional and motor centers, making it a potent tool for creating lasting memories. This brain activity is fueled by oxytocin, a chemical associated with empathy and trust.

Oxytocin levels rise when we engage with character-driven stories, prompting us to care about the characters and their situations. This neurological response also influences charitable donations, with people more likely to give when a story is involved. Moreover, shared storytelling experiences can foster empathy among diverse groups, reducing prejudice and promoting understanding. In fact, synthetic oxytocin, which enhances empathy, has been created, but the most potent "love potion" remains the art of storytelling.

Relatability

One of the key elements in effective storytelling is relatability, as seen in the iconic narrative of Star Wars. George Lucas, the creator, fused his love for fast cars, comic books, Kung Fu movies, and nostalgic sci-fi to craft a familiar yet captivating tale. This relatability is crucial because our brains are naturally drawn to the familiar. The mere-exposure theory in psychology suggests that exposure to something increases our liking for it over time. Companies like BuzzFeed understand this concept and use relatability to capture the attention of specific segments of society, resulting in viral stories.

Character-driven stories are particularly powerful because we see ourselves in these characters. Even villains can resonate with us when we recognize our own flaws in them. For instance, Darth Vader's journey in Star Wars taps into our understanding of the internal struggle between good and evil within ourselves.

The success of the Star Wars franchise illustrates the importance of maintaining relatability and natural nostalgia in storytelling. New elements introduced in the prequels felt forced, diminishing their appeal, while the latest sequels wisely incorporated old characters, themes, and plotlines, rekindling audience affection and generating significant revenue. The stories that endure and continue to captivate us are those that connect us to our past.

Novelty

The movie industry's obsession with sequels prompted an investigation into their performance and audience preference. The study revealed an interesting pattern: successful movies tend to have sequels that make less money and are liked less by audiences, especially after the third or fourth installment. There are two main types of sequels: "repeats" like Zoolander 2, which rehash the same elements, and "sagas" like Star Wars, which expand the storyline with new elements.

Great stories need to be novel, as our brains are naturally drawn to new experiences. Repeating the same story or content diminishes its impact and engagement, even if the quality remains constant. Original content, whether in movies or stories, often leads to more significant profits and a transformative impact. Relatability, characterized by familiar themes and characters, is crucial for engaging audiences, and creating memorable characters is a highly effective approach.

Tension

Tension is the element that transforms a good story into a great one. It captivates the audience, keeping them engaged and invested in the narrative.

The power of tension lies in creating a gap between what is and what a character desires. Aristotle's storytelling framework emphasizes this concept, where the storyteller's role is to bridge this gap and open new ones, thereby generating tension.

For instance, in the greatest love stories like Romeo and Juliet, there is intense tension due to obstacles and conflicts. Star Wars excels at this too, with family conflicts, planet destruction, and character deaths adding layers of tension. Striking a balance is crucial; too much tension can deter the audience, while no tension fails to engage them. Regardless of the story you are telling, be it a gardening blog or a thrilling action novel, remember that tension is a vital ingredient for maintaining audience attention.

Fluency

The reading level at which we write can impact our storytelling effectiveness. Writers often aim for higher reading levels, believing it conveys intelligence. However, this perception is challenged when assessing the reading levels of renowned writers, like Ernest Hemingway or J.K. Rowling, who actually write at lower reading levels.

This concept of "fluency" suggests that great storytelling should focus on simplicity rather than complexity. High reading levels can distract from the story, characters, tension, and the overall experience. Successful stories, like "Star Wars," are designed for quick comprehension, emphasizing fluid movement and minimal distractions.

In today's world, where attention spans are debated, the key for storytellers is to ensure each part of the story flows seamlessly to the next. Whether on social media, in writing, film, or casual conversations, fluency should be the priority, rather than aiming for complexity or intelligence in vocabulary and style.

Storytelling for relationship building in business

Commencing with a story has the remarkable ability to captivate the audience's attention, regardless of the presentation's topic. Additionally, I utilize a technique I learned from Guy Kawasaki, a prominent business leader and former Apple evangelist. Guy's method involves initiating each presentation with a personal story and a related photo, even if the story is not directly linked to the presentation's subject. The key insight here is that sharing a personal story at the outset of your presentation enhances the audience's connection with you and heightens their engagement. Whether you are a business leader delivering a speech, attempting to make a persuasive sales pitch, or conducting a routine workplace status update meeting, initiating your presentation with a story is one of the most powerful techniques to draw your audience in.

Using story to make more effective presentations

A few years ago, researchers at Johns Hopkins University analyzed Super Bowl ads to determine the key elements that led to audience appreciation and successful outcomes. They examined factors like cute animals, appearance appeal, and humor. Surprisingly, they found that regardless of these factors, the most highly-rated ads were those with compelling narrative arcs – essentially, they were stories. This aligns with the psychological and neurological perspective on storytelling, where facts and figures do not stick in our minds as effectively as stories. So, for advertisers looking to create memorable messages, storytelling is more potent than other approaches, including humor or using cute animals.

This is why content marketing, a concept that has gained immense popularity, is so powerful. It is a practice that businesses have used throughout history to build relationships that foster genuine care. Even seemingly uninteresting companies can humanize themselves by highlighting the personal stories of their employees. While these stories may not directly relate to the company's products or services, they make both the company and its staff relatable. Ultimately, your company's story, its founding myth, and the reasons behind its existence are more compelling than just discussing what you sell. Yes, your business aims to make a profit, but the underlying story of why you are doing it holds more value in building relationships that truly matter.

Selling and marketing yourself or your products

Groupon, one of the fastest-growing businesses in history, achieved its success through storytelling. When it launched in the late 2000s, it used storytelling as a clever marketing strategy. Groupon hired comedy writers from The Second City in Chicago to craft amusing fictional stories for each coupon they sent. This had two notable effects. Firstly, people were more likely to open Groupon emails because they anticipated the entertaining stories inside, even though they knew the stories were humorous but fake. Secondly, the stories were so engaging that recipients shared them with friends, resulting in increased Groupon sales and rapid growth.

Selling and marketing through storytelling is a highly effective method to boost conversion rates. It also makes your product more memorable for potential future purchases. This approach is prevalent in e-commerce and offline commerce today. Companies are leveraging the power of product stories to influence consumers' choices, even more so than price and quality.

When you have something to sell, do not just focus on the story of how someone might use your product or why it is excellent. Instead, explore the story behind the product. Explore the narrative of why you created it, how it was made, and who was involved in its creation. This story will connect with people and leave a lasting impression, making them remember your product more effectively. We at my company frequently discover products we appreciate and share the stories behind them.

The power of putting story into what you make and sell

General Electric (GE) invested millions of dollars in redesigning a new MRI machine for brain and body scans. However, when the inventor saw a frightened child about to undergo an MRI scan, he realized how terrifying the experience was for young patients. To address this issue, GE decided to use storytelling to transform the MRI experience for children. They painted the MRI machine like a pirate ship, provided kids with a storybook about a pirate adventure, and involved medical staff in pirate-themed attire. This narrative-driven approach changed children's perception of the MRI machine from fear and resistance to enthusiasm.

This story illustrates the power of storytelling. In the case of GE, a positive story enhanced the product's appeal and made it more child-friendly without requiring an expensive redesign. When consumers choose products or businesses, they consider factors like convenience, cost, quality, and personal preference. However, a compelling story embedded within a product can override these factors, making customers select something they may find less comfortable, but more enjoyable, due to the engaging narrative.

Understanding audience

When using storytelling for business, you have two key objectives: first, you need to reach an audience, and second, you want to cultivate and retain that audience. To achieve this, it's essential to comprehend who your audience is and what they desire. Religious parables offer a useful example of achieving this. They spoke in terms relevant to the people of their time. Just as discussing sheep or fish may not resonate with today's audience, these parables made sense back in the day when these were relatable. Similarly, modern business analogies should align with contemporary perspectives to effectively connect with and build your audience. This involves understanding their vocabulary, which is the obvious part. For instance, addressing credit union members correctly. On the less obvious side, understanding the white space is crucial.

As our society faces a constant influx of content and stories, it's essential for storytellers to identify opportunities for offering something unique and valuable. Utilize data, Venn diagrams, social media insights, or explore interconnected interests to identify these opportunities. Recognize that your audience is not one-dimensional. Even in B2B contexts, remember that your audience is human and possesses multifaceted interests. Consider the people and topics they care about, not just the products they might desire. Building and maintaining an audience is a pivotal part of contemporary business growth. Once you have an audience, their loyalty becomes a valuable asset. They will follow you, listen to your future messages, and engage with your brand. Consistently nurturing this audience is the key to long-term success in the modern business landscape. As Martin Luther King wisely noted, "If I stopped preaching to the choir, they'll stop singing."

The story-relationship funnel

When using stories to build relationships, the type of stories you tell depends on the stage of the relationship, much like dating. In the initial stages, you discuss common interests and safe topics, avoiding personal or intimate stories. As the relationship progresses, you can explore more personal and meaningful stories.

To help generate story ideas for this relationship-building process, you can use a funnel matrix with three dimensions based on timeliness:

1. Extremely Timely Stories: These are about current events or topics of immediate relevance, sharing common values between you and your audience.

2. Seasonal Stories: Focused on events or seasons, they relate to specific time frames or occasions.

3. Timeless Stories (Evergreen): These stories are relevant at any time and help build a long-lasting connection with your audience.

Consider where your relationship stands and use the concept of timeliness to brainstorm stories that match that stage. Different businesses may utilize these dimensions based on their specific relationships with their audiences:

- American Express, for instance, shares timely stories related to the economy, showing shared concerns with small business owners.

- General Electric (GE) tells evergreen stories about their employees and their projects, creating a lasting connection.

- Groupon shares timely stories about its products, often with humor, focusing on the deeper story behind each coupon.

This matrix allows you to tailor your storytelling to the relationship stage and the level of timeliness required, enabling creative and effective storytelling at each phase of your audience engagement.

The story matrix

Storytelling relies on reaching and engaging your audience effectively. To achieve this, you can visualize your strategy as a "storytelling bullseye." The bullseye consists of two main categories: business storytelling and consumer storytelling, with two goals in mind - awareness/branding or action/conversion.

At the very center of the bullseye is your own website, which works well for all goals and audiences. Next, consider your email list, which allows you to share stories directly with your audience. If neither your website nor email is accessible to your target audience, you should reach them on their turf.

Here is a breakdown of platforms based on your goal and audience:

1. LinkedIn: Ideal for business storytelling aimed at perception or branding.

2. YouTube: Suitable for consumer storytelling when focusing on perception or branding.

3. SlideShare: Effective for business storytelling when your goal is to drive actions.

4. Pinterest: Great for consumer storytelling, particularly if you want people to take action.

Regardless of the platform, your stories should guide your audience deeper into your bullseye. Use calls to action that encourage them to subscribe or explore more stories on your website or via email. The goal is to progressively pull your audience closer to your turf, ultimately building your own loyal audience.

Create, connect, optimize

Throughout history, there's been a consistent pattern for building audiences through storytelling. It starts with creating content and connecting with the audience. In the Renaissance era, gossip writers collected and distributed stories in newsletters, optimizing their approach to reach more people.

In the 1800s, newspapers battled for attention by using sensational headlines. Joseph Pulitzer revolutionized the industry by hiring investigative journalist Nellie Bly, who explored deep, meaningful stories that built audience loyalty.

Fast forward to Upworthy, a modern media company that accelerated this process. They tested and optimized stories by repackaging them with new headlines and images, continually refining until they found the most engaging version. Then they shared the story with their audience via email and their website.

Today, technology enables you to create, connect, and optimize more efficiently than ever before. With just an internet connection, you can harness the power of this storytelling flywheel.

Unleashing potential energy

Building an audience through storytelling is akin to building lasting relationships – it takes repeated interactions. Consistent storytelling offers compounding returns, similar to a snowball effect. To illustrate this, consider two YouTube stars who went viral in the same month.

Michelle Phan, a makeup artist, gained fame for her "Bad Romance" makeup video. Her success did not happen overnight; it was her 50th YouTube story. Her channel offered a stream of captivating content, drawing a strong, loyal fan base.

In contrast, Bear Vasquez, known for the "Double Rainbow" video, could not replicate his initial success. He lacked a library of engaging content and faltered with subsequent videos.

The key takeaway: building an audience involves continuous storytelling and improving your stories over time. It is not a one-time endeavor, but with persistence, the results can be remarkable, just like consistent effort at the gym leads to improved fitness.

Universal storytelling frameworks

The hero's journey, a storytelling template by Joseph Campbell, is a recurring pattern seen in numerous stories. It consists of various stages: starting in an ordinary world, receiving a call to adventure, initial refusal, meeting a wise mentor, crossing the threshold into an adventure, facing trials, finding allies and enemies, approaching a final battle, almost losing, succeeding, receiving a reward, and returning home transformed with new powers or objects.

For example, in "Star Wars," Luke Skywalker starts on a desert planet, meets Obi-Wan Kenobi, is trained to save the universe, and ultimately conquers the Death Star, receiving the Force and a lightsaber as his reward.

Aristotle's story structure is simpler, establishing what is, what could be, and creating tension between the two. This structure is useful for case studies in business storytelling.

Additionally, Dan Harmon's storytelling template, often used in comedy writing, involves a character in a zone of comfort who seeks something, enters an unfamiliar situation, adapts, acquires what they want at a price, and returns changed to their familiar situation.

These frameworks are versatile tools for crafting engaging stories in various contexts, tapping into the universal human journey. They provide structure and guidance, making storytelling more creative and accessible.

The Ben Franklin method

Benjamin Franklin, a renowned figure in history, struggled with writing at one point in his life. To improve his skills, he devised a method. He would take articles from a prestigious magazine, "The Spectator," and describe them in his own words, sentence by sentence. After a few days, he had rewritten the article from his notes and compare it to the original to identify mistakes and areas for improvement. This process continued until he believed his writing surpassed the original. Inspired by this, I used a similar approach to enhance my own writing skills. Many of us may not view ourselves as great writers, but like Franklin, we can use this method to become better storytellers, regardless of our current abilities.

The sludge report

The "sludge report" is collectively trimming paragraphs by eliminating wordy phrases, known as "sludge words." This approach challenges writers to make their points succinct. The key is to use shorter words to convey your message effectively. George Orwell believed in this, saying, "Why use a long word when you can use a short word?" So, when you write, assess each paragraph, aiming to make it half as long, using the sludge method to enhance your writing's quality, keeping the focus on the story.

Creating a culture of storytelling

Storytelling can positively impact how teams, partnerships, and companies collaborate. Research reveals that sharing personal stories breaks down barriers and forges connections, particularly among diverse individuals. To foster a storytelling culture, consider the following: First, ensure your teams have individuals with unique stories, as these stories signify a diversity of thought and perspectives, influencing problem-solving approaches. Additionally, employ stories as responses to interview questions, as they effectively convey a person's character and problem-solving skills. Lastly, promote the sharing of personal stories within teams, as this enhances trust, openness, and encourages quieter individuals to speak up. Stories are a powerful tool to connect and build relationships, transforming how people work and live. Great stories have the potential to change not only individual lives but the world as well, so let's share our remarkable stories.

Chapter 4 Creating and Giving Business Presentations

Identify your audience's knowledge level

Have you ever been in an audience feeling lost because the speaker either assumes you know too little or too much about the topic? This occurs when speakers do not consider what their audience knows. To bridge this gap, simplify your explanation for a less informed audience, relate unfamiliar topics to what they know, and avoid jargon. When your audience is familiar, you can use insider language. If your audience is a mix of knowledge levels, address both. Research your audience's knowledge or arrive early to clarify. Ensure your presentation caters to everyone's understanding to make it smooth and engaging.

Why should your audience care?

"Show me the money" is a phrase often used to mean getting straight to the point or understanding the benefits. When addressing an audience, whether they're motivated by curiosity or obligation, you must immediately communicate the value to them. To do this effectively, you need a deep understanding of what drives them, whether it is success, recognition, profit, or other factors. Talk to those who know your audience well and gather information before your presentation. If possible, engage with your audience beforehand to understand their expectations. Tailor your presentation to their preferences and values, whether it is financial benefits or non-monetary impacts.

Preconceived notions about your topic can vary, so it is crucial to manage these perceptions. Make sure you align your message with the audience's values. By being well-prepared, you can anticipate the audience's needs and address the "so what" question without them having to ask.

Prepare for your audience's reactions

When delivering a message, the audience can be ready, apathetic, or skeptical. To be an effective speaker, adjust your approach according to their reaction. Here are some tips for each situation:

- For a receptive audience, engage them by showing your investment in the information and encouraging dialogue.

- With an apathetic audience, use attention-grabbers and communicate the value of your message.

- When facing a resistant audience, address their concerns, have answers ready, and allow early dialogue.

Know your audience's communication style

To engage your audience effectively, consider these communication style differences:

1. Big Picture vs. Details: Determine whether your audience prefers an overview (the "forest") or in-depth information (the "trees"). Some groups like specifics and detailed charts, while others want to see the broader picture first and how it aligns with the organization's mission.

2. Formality Levels: Companies have varying levels of formality. When presenting, adapt your style based on your audience's expectations. When unsure, err on the side of formality. Spend time with the organization's members before your presentation to gauge the appropriate level.

3. Interruptions: Know if your audience typically engages in two-way conversations with intermittent questions during presentations. Plan for frequent check-ins and encourage interaction, but clarify this with your audience before you start speaking.

4. Facts vs. Emotion: Consider whether your audience prefers starting with a direct fact or an emotional approach, such as a story or local fable that connects to the main point. Be flexible in your approach, especially if you're accustomed to presenting facts.

5. Language: When presenting to a non-native English-speaking audience, simplify your language, avoid acronyms, idioms, casual expressions, and colloquialisms. Speak clearly, pace yourself, and ensure your pronunciation is precise.

To maintain your credibility, understand your audience's communication style by asking questions and conducting early research. By considering these factors, you will be better prepared to connect with your audience effectively.

Build credibility

A speaker's credibility encompasses perceptions, actions, and behaviors. Consider how you appear to your audience in each aspect.

1. Perceptions: If you're an outsider to a group, have someone from within the organization introduce you. Alternatively, connect with audience members before your presentation, learn about their interests, and tailor your presentation accordingly to manage the perception of being an outsider.

2. Credible Actions: Your credibility is evident in the energy, punctuality, and quality of interactions before and after your presentation. It's also demonstrated by the depth and relevance of your research on the topic. Avoid hedging words and use strong, factual language.

3. Non-Verbals: Non-verbal communication, including body language, gestures, facial expressions, and tone of voice, plays a crucial role in conveying credibility. Your interest in the topic, firm handshake, open body language, confidence, and eye contact all contribute to your professional brand.

Your presentation should reflect and enhance your brand, showcasing your expertise and ability to connect with the audience. Think of your professional brand as your character, and ensure your credibility aligns with it.

Collect your information

"Less is more" is a principle of focus and efficiency in presentations. Achieving this requires several strategic steps:

1. Start with a brainstorming session to list all potential information your audience might want.

2. Seek clarifications from your contact or a colleague to narrow down your list.

3. Identify common themes and group related topics while recognizing outliers.

4. Conduct additional research to support the themes.

5. Narrow your focus by selecting a few key items that align with your initial charge and are well-supported.

Follow these steps to concentrate on a few essential points, allowing your audience to grasp your message clearly. Achieving the "less is more" approach may require multiple steps, but it is a valuable endeavor.

Create logical appeal

The logical appeal of your presentation involves visual and verbal design elements that aid your audience in recalling your main message and supporting points. Think of it as the roadmap for your message, guiding your audience to the destination. To enhance your logical appeal, consider the following:

1. Ensure your presentation's hook ties back to the close.

2. Mention your theme consistently throughout the presentation.

3. Sequence your main points logically with smooth transitions.

4. Support each main point with solid evidence, such as statistics, studies, graphs, and surveys from recent, credible sources.

5. Conclude by outlining next steps or additional resources, offering your audience a clear path forward.

By following these steps, you can strengthen the logical appeal of your presentation, making you a sought-after speaker for your organization.

Use emotion

Aristotle once said, "Educating the mind without educating the heart is no education at all." As you prepare for your upcoming presentation, consider these ways to engage the heart:

1. Leverage body language by maintaining an open, upright posture, using expressive gestures, maintaining eye contact, and leaning toward the audience.

2. Vary your voice by altering pitch, volume, and rate of speech to convey energy and emotion.

3. Speak with conviction, maintaining a positive tone and showcasing confidence in your topic.

4. Adapt the intensity of emotion to match the audience's context and expectations.

5. Utilize facial expressions to convey emotions like surprise, fear, and concern, as non-verbal communicate meaning quickly.

To evoke emotion, share captivating stories and examples related to your central theme, ensuring they resonate with your audience. Choose visually engaging and vivid language to describe situations or individuals. Consider language tools like alliteration, antithesis, repetition, and humor if they suit the context and your comfort level.

As you wrap up the organization stage of your presentation, make a list of ways to incorporate both logic and emotion into your content effectively.

Organize your content

Think of a well-organized presentation like a beautifully wrapped gift. Just like you want to open a present with an enticing bow and wrapping, your audience should be eager to explore your content. To achieve this, focus on these key elements for a memorable presentation:

1. Begin with Impact: Start with a captivating opening that grabs your audience's attention. Use relevant statistics, stories, or real-world examples that connect with their needs and interests. Your energy and confidence are vital in this part.

2. Preview the Journey: Introduce your main theme and provide a brief overview of what's coming. Ensure your main points are logically sequenced and easy for the audience to follow.

3. Establish Credibility: Subtly highlight the work you've done in preparing for the presentation, such as talking to experts, reading reports, or drawing from your relevant experience.

4. Seamless Transitions: As you move through your main points, maintain smooth transitions between them. Conclude each point with a summary and a logical connection to the next one.

5. Confident Closure: End your presentation with confidence and energy. Summarize your main points and relate them back to the engaging opening. You can also mention next steps or transition to a Q&A session.

Your presentation is a gift to your audience, so captivate them from the beginning and gradually unwrap your well-organized content.

Sketch your presentation

When planning your presentation, begin with a pen and paper, not PowerPoint or Keynote. Structure your presentation into three simple parts: introduction, body, and conclusion.

Introduction:

- Grab your audience's attention visually.

- Establish your expertise through your research.

- Introduce your theme using facts or a story.

- Preview the main points and create smooth transitions.

Body:

- For each main point, outline subpoints and provide supporting evidence.

- Keep your theme woven throughout to maintain a cohesive message.

Conclusion:

- Summarize your main points.

- Encourage action or transition to a Q&A session if necessary.

Practice handling interruptions during the presentation if Q&A is ongoing.

Develop slide and images

Once you have outlined your presentation, the next step is designing your slides. Consider the following key points as you create your slides:

1. Nail the Intro Slide:

   - Make a positive first impression with a professional, compelling intro slide.

   - It represents your brand, hints at your main message, and reminds the audience of your identity.

2. Strategize Slide Background and Design:

   - Determine if you must use a company template or if you have design flexibility.

   - Create a fresh visual template, incorporating your theme and maintaining a consistent color scheme.

   - Prioritize clarity, avoid text clutter, and use relevant, concise slide titles.

   - Find the right balance between images and text, considering your organization's visual culture.

3. Use Animation Thoughtfully:

   - Utilize meaningful animations that enhance content.

   - Avoid cramming images into corners and use animation that aligns with your message.

- Keep slides uncluttered, using them as visual aids, not cheat sheets.

4. Keep It Simple and Organized:

  - Reflect your clear message and logical flow on slides.

  - Show a preview of your points and include a visual agenda for easy navigation.

  - Manage data effectively, using animations to highlight key elements and hyperlinking for additional information.

By following this strategic design process, you can receive positive feedback from your audience.

Build your deck

Every presentation is unique, tailored to the specific needs of your audience and organization.

1. Introduction Slide:

  - Introduce the presentation theme and provide an overview.

2. Entering Slide:

  - Preview main points: building connections, relationships, credibility, and patience.

3. Connections Slide:

  - Discuss research on uncertainty avoidance.

  - Emphasize the importance of forming personal connections and open body language.

4. Relationships Slide:

  - Cover key opportunities for building relationships, such as regional and local trade shows.

5. Patience Slide:

  - Reference relevant reports or data supporting the need for patience in the context of your presentation.

6. Closing Slide:

  - Feature your organization's logo and highlight your main message.

  - Summarize the key points of your presentation.

7. Q&A Slide:

  - Prepare for the question-and-answer session.

Feel free to adapt this template to your specific presentation, audience, and organization.

Make edits

Now, it is time for the editing phase. Seek a trusted colleague's assistance to fine-tune your presentation visuals. Share the presentation's scope, describe the audience, and your desired outcomes. If you are not in the same location, share the visuals online but ensure to explain the context. Run through the main points without a full rehearsal and request feedback on flow, visuals, and the Q&A section.

For each slide, ask your colleague the following:

1. Was the initial slide descriptive?

2. Were the colors, fonts, spacing, and visuals appealing?

3. Did any slides appear confusing?

4. Did you maintain pace throughout, or were there moments you fell behind?

5. Could you identify a recurring theme or remember the main points?

6. Did the information flow logically?

Additionally, if your colleague is familiar with the topic or audience, ask if they can suggest potential Q&A questions. If the presentation is shared electronically, ensure that bullet points and notes capture your message effectively. Finally, inquire if your colleague recommends any supplementary handouts. Remember, feedback helps refine your presentation, so be open to constructive changes.

Practice makes perfect

In his book "Outliers," Malcolm Gladwell discusses the 10,000-hour rule as the time required to master a skill. He emphasizes that with dedication and hard work, anyone can excel at something. The art of delivering presentations is a skill you can master through passionate and detailed preparation. Here are some tips:

1. Practice both formally and informally. Share your presentation overview with a colleague for feedback, discuss your topic with your family, or leave a voicemail with an opening. Develop cues to remember key points in the right order.

2. Perform a dry run in the same setting as your actual presentation, using the same equipment. Time yourself or consider audio and video recording to identify areas for improvement.

3. Include visuals in your practice, especially for complex points or challenging names and figures. Use visuals to your advantage and maintain confidence.

4. Practice in sections, focusing on the introduction, individual points, and the conclusion. Avoid practicing continuously from start to finish.

5. Practice your content in three segments: from the introduction to the first point, from the second point to the review of the third point, and then the overall review, closing, and Q&A transition.

6. Time yourself during practice to ensure you stay within your allotted time. Always leave ample time for the Q&A session, as going a little short is preferable to going over time.

While not recommending spending 10,000 hours practicing, embrace the idea that practice brings you closer to perfection, following Malcolm Gladwell's principle.

Calming nerves

It is important to note that not all stress is negative; we all have different stress tolerances and responses during peak performance.

Here are some techniques to consider:

1. Embrace a healthy level of nervousness in your stomach.

2. Use controlled breathing to calm and center yourself, especially during pauses between sentences.

3. Practice in a heightened state, such as after running upstairs, to become more comfortable with increased heart rate.

4. Desensitize your brain by practicing in the actual presentation space.

5. Practice in attire similar to what you'll wear on the big day.

6. Arrive early on the presentation day, set up your technology, and engage in small talk with attendees.

7. Visualize yourself speaking confidently and successfully in front of the audience.

8. Prepare for technology issues with backup plans, extra batteries, and materials.

9. Watch your caffeine intake, stay hydrated, and maintain a balanced diet.

10. Shift your focus from self-concern to meeting your audience's needs, becoming a facilitator for their solutions. This shift in perspective can improve your presentation.

Remember, speaking anxiety can be managed effectively by using these sports-related techniques and strategies.

Smart use of space

"Own your space" means appearing confident and experienced when you present. Whether standing in front of an audience or sitting at a conference table, good posture and controlled movement are essential. Maintain a strong and relaxed posture, keeping your shoulders square to the audience. Avoid swaying, shifting weight, or shuffling around. When sitting in a chair, sit at the edge, engage your core muscles, and keep your chest lifted to prevent slouching.

Effective movement involves using available space strategically. However, movement may be limited at a podium. Use gestures to convey energy, and if possible, step away from the podium for a powerful closing statement. Be mindful of not blocking projector lights. Practice in the presentation room and remember that strong posture and controlled movement project confidence during your presentation.

Gestures that engage

When it comes to what to do with your hands while speaking, remember this: less is more. Keep your hands relaxed by your sides or on the conference table to convey a sense of calm and confidence. While you should use gestures when necessary to match your words and emotions, avoid overdoing it, as excessive hand-waving can be distracting.

Appropriate gestures can serve three purposes: they add energy to your delivery, emphasize key points, and help the audience remember. Use gestures when discussing people in the room or far-off places, explaining timelines, numbers, or processes. Repeating certain gestures can make their meaning clear to the audience.

Some gestures can enhance your message, but there are unhelpful ones to avoid, like hand-wringing, pocket-holding, or excessive fidgeting. Remember that notes can aid your memory, but be cautious not to overuse them or let them distract from your connection with the audience.

Use gestures thoughtfully, and practice using them in everyday conversations if you are not comfortable. The key is to strike a balance that complements your message without becoming a distraction.

Strategic eye contact

Confident and culturally appropriate eye contact is a valuable asset in effective speaking. Successful speakers establish a comfortable connection with their audience by scanning them while making intentional eye-to-eye contact. Meaningful eye contact involves remembering the color of someone's eyes, not fleeting glances that convey urgency.

Here are some tips if maintaining eye contact with a group makes you nervous:

1. Follow the three-second rule: Look at each person for at least three seconds while making your points, avoiding constant scanning.

2. Focus on friendly faces: Engage with audience members who provide positive nonverbal feedback through smiling, nodding, or verbal confirmation. Don't let disinterested individuals distract you.

3. Practice maintaining eye contact at eye level: In the United States, eye contact signifies confidence and credibility. Practice this skill in everyday interactions, like at a checkout counter or while ordering coffee.

4. Practice in the presentation room: Utilize screens with faces looking at you or visual landmarks in empty audience seats to simulate a real audience.

Eye contact is a powerful nonverbal tool that conveys interest, confidence, trust, and a willingness to connect with your audience. Use these practice tips to improve your eye contact skills for effective speaking.

Opening and closing strong

The beginnings and endings of your presentations serve as crucial bookends. They strategically capture the audience's attention, enhance your credibility, issue a call to action, and leave a lasting impression. To maintain logical appeal, always link your opening to the closing.

Here is how you can engage your audience effectively:

1. Begin with a relevant quote, statistic, or newspaper tagline that tightly connects to your audience's interests.

2. If you choose to open with a story, make it sensory-rich by describing vivid details like images, colors, settings, feelings, and more.

3. Asking a question, whether directed at the audience or yourself, breaks monotony and increases engagement. Use questions in your introduction with a well-placed pause to build intrigue.

4. Encourage audience participation through show of hands or nods to create a connection.

5. If you started with an open-ended question, reference it in your closing and tie it to the points you've shared, possibly concluding with a call to action or a clear request.

Incorporate these elements into your presentation to create strong bookends, where your energy is high, and your message is crystal clear.

Holding a Q&A session

The Q&A section is your moment to excel. Allocate sufficient time for it, as being well-prepared will enhance your relationship with the audience and boost your credibility. During this segment, you can connect, inform, and inspire:

1. Connect: Encourage questions by summarizing your content and transitioning to Q&A smoothly. Show attentive listening by paraphrasing or repeating questions and respond while involving the entire audience. For off-topic or complex questions, redirect or break them down.

2. Inform: Prepare for the Q&A just as thoroughly as your presentation. Anticipate questions, practice with others, and have extra material ready for in-depth answers. Be patient with silence and steer the conversation if needed.

3. Inspire: Reinforce your main points and stay organized during responses. Keep the discussion relevant and, if time allows, end with a brief closing statement that emphasizes your key message.

Practice a mock Q&A with a checklist to improve your speaking skills. Though it may seem intense initially, commitment to the process will make you a better speaker.

Sharpen your skills

Enhancing your speaking skills requires constant feedback and practice. Here is a progression from simple to more advanced techniques:

1. Record a voicemail message: If you struggle with flat intonation, rambling, and fillers, practice by leaving a voicemail to yourself. Listen for improvements and repeat until you or a trusted friend notices progress.

2. Videotape yourself: Use your smartphone to record your practice or live presentations. Analyze the recording by watching it three times:

  - First, focus on your physicality and interactions.

  - Second, listen to your voice for energy, conviction, pauses, and varied intonation.

  - Third, take a holistic view, considering context and content. Create a list of strengths and areas for improvement, and share it with a colleague or family member for confirmation.

3. Create an action plan: Set realistic, measurable goals based on areas for improvement. For example, work on your speaking pace by measuring your words per minute, aiming for 150 to 200 words per minute. Use pauses strategically, record your progress, and expect changes to take about six weeks.

4. Step out of your comfort zone: Attend a Toastmasters International Club meeting for regular speaking practice. Participate actively in work meetings to share updates and reflections. Look for non-work speaking opportunities like addressing a sports team, making toasts, or giving speeches at social gatherings.

Continuous practice, feedback, and seizing speaking opportunities are keys to improving your speaking skills.

Chapter 5 Create and Deliver Standout Technical Presentations

Audience-centric speaking

In presentations, we often focus on ourselves, our goals, comfort, and interests, known as "speaker-centric speaking." This can involve cluttered slides, technical jargon, and emphasizing personal preferences. However, our success as speakers depends on making our audience successful, which we achieve through "audience-centric speaking." To excel in this approach, we continually ask, "What makes sense for my audience?" This question guides content, slides, and delivery choices, even if it means stepping out of our comfort zone. To understand your audience better, consider: Who are they? What do they know? Why are they here? What do they care about? By prioritizing the audience's needs over our own, we ensure success in our presentations.

Overcoming audience bias

Have you ever presented to an audience that seemed closed-minded from the start, showing little interest in your information? Overcoming audience bias is a common challenge for technical speakers. Bias can take different forms, such as technical or programmatic bias. The problem arises when speakers attempt to overcome bias by bombarding the audience with facts, like throwing them at a brick wall. However, this approach is often ineffective.

Instead, a more successful strategy, as suggested by communication expert Michael Alley, is to acknowledge the bias openly. When you name the bias and express awareness of your audience's concerns, it lowers the metaphorical wall of resistance. This approach fosters a collaborative, receptive atmosphere, making the audience more curious and open to the information you're sharing. In essence, acknowledging bias changes the dynamic of the presentation from defensive to collaborative, facilitating a more effective communication process.

Reaching experts and nonexperts

A challenging but common audience for technical speakers is the diverse one, comprising both experts and non-experts. Balancing their needs might seem difficult, as you need to provide enough technical information for the experts without overwhelming the non-experts. The key strategy here is to identify "points of common ground," which are concepts everyone can grasp, regardless of their background.

While many presenters start with these points, the problem arises when they explore deep into technical details and never resurface. To succeed with a diverse audience, it is crucial to be a "snorkeler of the science." Just like a snorkeler can dive but needs to come up for air, you should provide technical details and then use "snorkel statements" to explain the practical significance. These statements clarify the "so what" of your technical information, connecting it to the audience's interests. By doing this, you become an interpreter of your work, not just a reporter, which resonates more with diverse audiences of both experts and non-experts, driving change and gaining their buy-in.

Filtering technical detail

In my numerous discussions with key stakeholders in technical industries, including executives, managers, funders, and end users, a common issue they raise about technical presentations is overwhelming detail. Presenters often try to cover too much in a single presentation, which can result in confusion and disengagement among the audience. Effective technical communication requires the ability to filter and focus on the essential details.

Think of yourself as a navigator in a presentation, guiding the audience toward a specific destination, which is what you want them to understand about your subject. To avoid overwhelming your audience, start your content planning with the end goal in mind. Ask yourself, "Where do I want my audience to be at the end of this presentation? What do they need to believe or understand for it to be a success?"

For instance, if your goal is for the audience to understand the need for new methods to detect pancreatic cancer, you identify key details: understanding the seriousness of pancreatic cancer and the inadequacy of current detection methods. Writing down your main message and identifying these key points will improve your ability to convince stakeholders of your ideas and recommendations. Clarity is convincing, while confusion is costly.

Heads vs. hearts: Connecting with emotions

Dale Carnegie once stated that when dealing with people, you are not addressing creatures of logic, but creatures of emotion. Yet, many recent technical presentations mainly deliver facts, figures, findings, and recommendations without evoking any emotional response. These presentations often miss the chance to connect with the audience on an emotional level, aside from the analytical side.

It is a common misconception that emotions have no place in scientific presentations. However, emotions play a crucial role in human experiences, decision-making, and connection with others. Emotions help us filter and prioritize information, making it more memorable and relevant. As a technical communicator, harnessing emotions is a valuable tool to engage your audience effectively.

It is not about choosing between logic and emotion, but rather striking a balance. In many technical presentations, the focus is primarily on logic, but a more strategic use of emotion can enhance their effectiveness. You can incorporate emotion through storytelling, analogies, or compelling visuals, achieving a better balance in your technical communication. This approach ensures that you are reaching the whole human, engaging both their intellect and emotions, as actions are often driven by emotions. Utilize this strategy in your next presentation to become more compelling.

Challenging the status quo: Why bullet points do not work

PowerPoint slides have become synonymous with presentations, often overshadowing the speaker's role. Many meetings and conferences bombard audiences with text-heavy, crowded slides featuring bullet lists. Common problems with these slides include excessive text, small fonts, poor color choices, and unclear main points.

The typical slide design, with a title and a bulleted list, dates back to the early versions of PowerPoint's default master template in the late 1980s. This design was originally created for the convenience of speakers, without considering how audiences learn and process information. Research on how people learn and process information has not been integrated into these text-heavy slides, which are fundamentally designed for the presenter, not the audience.

To stand out and make your ideas more effective, consider rethinking the way you design slides. By focusing on audience needs and learning principles, you can make your presentations more impactful and break free from the flawed tradition of text-heavy slides.

Brain hacks for slide design

Slides play a crucial role in presentations as they are present throughout the entire presentation lifecycle. They affect how you prepare, deliver, and how well the audience understands your message. The typical approach to slide design prioritizes the presenter's perspective, but it is essential to shift the focus towards creating slides that are effective for the audience.

To enhance the effectiveness of your slides, consider two principles from cognitive psychology, which studies how people learn and process information. First, think about a typical presentation situation from the audience's perspective. Your brain, as an audience member, needs to process both what the speaker says and what's on the slide. However, it is impossible to simultaneously process both sets of information due to cognitive overload. Cognitive overload occurs when you exceed the brain's capacity to handle words-based information.

Think of your audience's brain as having two lanes for information input: one for words-based information and one for visual information. Traditional text-heavy slides often create a traffic jam on the words-based lane, while the visual lane remains open. Visual information is processed differently and more deeply in the brain, leading to a better understanding and retention of the content.

To design effective slides, consider the audience's cognitive abilities and leverage the picture superiority effect. Use more visual elements to support your verbal content, aligning with the way the human brain processes information.

The assertion-evidence slide design

Assertion Evidence design philosophy has helped numerous scientists, engineers, and technical professionals worldwide enhance their communication. primary research behind Assertion Evidence comes from Penn State University, particularly Professor Michael Alley, an expert in engineering communication.

The key change you will make in your slide design is transitioning from a phrase or topic as the headline to a concise take-away message. Instead of a vague topic, your goal is to answer the question, "What do I want my audience to know or take away from this slide?" and express it as a full sentence. This shift makes you think more deeply about your message and results in more focused and understandable slides. The take-away message gives you immediate clarity for the rest of your slide's content.

Moreover, to transform your slide design, you wll support your take-away message with visual evidence. Visual evidence encompasses various elements such as illustrations, pictures, graphs, diagrams, and more. It's important to avoid bulleted lists as they can be confusing and fail to represent the relationships between pieces of information effectively. Instead, consider using diagrams to display these relationships, and if necessary, include text as call-outs or key features of your visual evidence.

The Assertion Evidence strategy involves creating a clear take-away message paired with suitable visual elements, resulting in more engaging and comprehensible technical slides. This approach marks a significant innovation in slide design, ensuring your ideas reach your audience's minds more effectively.

A template beyond bullet points

The starting point for your presentation is crucial. While many begin with the default template, which often leads to text-heavy bullet-point slides, I recommend using the assertion evidence template. You can easily find it by searching terms like "assertion evidence," "technical presentation," or "scientific presentation" when opening a new PowerPoint presentation. Pin it to have easy access for future use. Alternatively, you can visit templates.office.com, search for "assertion evidence" or "technical presentation," and download it for free.

Once you have the template, let's dive into how to use it effectively. The template provides suggested layouts with sample content to guide you. When starting a new presentation, do a "Save As" and give it your presentation name, then delete any example slides that are not relevant to your content. You can select a layout or create your own. However, I recommend maintaining the size and position of the headline but feel free to adjust the color and font to match your brand.

When adding content to the slide, remember to avoid bulleted lists. Instead, use text as call-outs or key features, as the template suggests. For your personal talking points, use the notes pages. The objective is to design your slides with your audience in mind.

By following these steps, you will create a slide with a clear message at the top and visual evidence on the body of the slide. It is far more engaging and informative than a typical bulleted slide.

Customize the template to align with your company or institution's branding by adjusting the colors and incorporating logos, typically placed in the bottom left corner. Consider sharing the template with your company's marketing team to establish it as a framework for a new corporate template. This can significantly improve presentations within your organization and reduce the reliance on bullet points.

Start your next presentation using this assertion evidence template to easily create focused, visually engaging slides that captivate your audience.

Creating a successful handout

How often have you felt compelled to overload your slides with details because they must stand alone when shared with absentees? It is a common problem, as we end up designing slides to serve as both presentation aids and comprehensive documentation. This dual role can undermine the effectiveness of our live presentations.

The key is to optimize slides for live presentations, focusing on visuals that complement the speaker's narrative. Then, leverage PowerPoint's Notes pages for capturing in-depth information. These Notes pages serve as an excellent solution when sharing the deck with those who could not attend or for future reference.

When you distribute a PDF with the Notes pages, your audience receives the best of both worlds. They see concise, visual slides with main takeaways during the live presentation, and the subsequent pages provide comprehensive details and references. This approach allows you to maintain the quality of the live presentation and create a valuable handout, all within the same PowerPoint file.

Gain attention with your title slide

In presentations, first impressions are crucial. Your audience quickly decides whether to pay attention or disengage. Many presenters start with generic title slides, missing the opportunity to captivate their audience. To make a better first impression, rethink your title slides.

For instance, consider a more engaging title slide with a relevant image and provide context or a story connected to the image. This approach immediately grabs the audience's interest and sets the tone for an engaging presentation. Start by engaging your audience from the very beginning, making them eager to hear more.

Make your agenda slide memorable

In presentations, it is essential to set the audience's expectations and create a memorable agenda slide. The typical agenda slide lacks impact and does not serve its purpose well. To make it more effective, follow these design principles:

1. Start with a meaningful topic or thesis statement at the top that captures the presentation's main focus.

2. Preview the two to four key points or sections of your presentation. Omit common sections like introductions or conclusions.

3. Include a visual image that matches the content of the first slide in each section. This helps the audience remember the presentation's structure.

4. For longer presentations, consider revisiting the agenda slide at transition points, highlighting the current section and graying out the others.

Creating a visual and engaging agenda slide ensures that your audience can follow the presentation and remember its key points. You might want to create the agenda slide after developing the rest of the presentation to ensure it aligns with the content.

Close with impact

At the end of a presentation, it is crucial to leave a lasting impact and avoid overwhelming or underwhelming conclusion slides. Typically, many presentations end with a slide labeled "Conclusions," "Questions," or "Thank You," which often fails to engage the audience effectively. To finish strong and close with impact:

1. Place your most important message at the top of the slide. Think of it as the one key takeaway you want your audience to remember.

2. Include two to three key messages from your presentation, emphasizing the journey to your destination message.

3. Use your best visual evidence from the presentation; do not introduce new content.

4. Animate the word "Questions" when you're ready for the Q&A session.

By adopting this approach, you provide an engaging and informative summary that helps the audience process the main points more easily. This type of conclusion slide can also prompt better questions during the Q&A session and keep the audience engaged even when not actively participating in the discussion.

Effective pace enhances credibility

To deliver a technically complex presentation effectively, consider the pace of your delivery. An ideal speaking pace falls in the range of 120 to 150 words per minute, but how do you measure this? Utilize the PowerPoint Presenter Coach, a feature that provides real-time feedback. Here's how:

1. Access Presenter Coach in PowerPoint's Slide Show tab, then click "Rehearse with Coach."

2. Begin practicing your presentation in slideshow mode while delivering it as you normally would.

3. After practice, end the slideshow to view your rehearsal report.

The report assesses various verbal aspects, including your speaking pace, highlighted in red. By practicing with this tool multiple times, you can develop a sense of the appropriate speaking rate and make it a habit for future presentations. To further gauge your pace, follow the "one slide per minute" rule, ensuring your slide count does not exceed the presentation time. Adjust your pace depending on the complexity of the content, slowing down for intricate details and accelerating for more conversational segments. Striking the right balance showcases confidence and ensures an engaging presentation. Use Presenter Coach and manage your slide count to achieve a successful speaking pace in your technical presentations.

Engage your audience with eye contact

Effective presentations require meaningful eye contact, as it helps in establishing a connection with the audience and allows you to gauge their engagement. Consider these tips for both in-person and virtual presentations:

In-Person Presentations:

- For genuine eye contact, look at individual audience members rather than scanning their heads.

- If you blank out when making eye contact, do not panic; take a deep breath, regain your thoughts, and continue.

Developing Eye Contact Skills:

- To become more comfortable with eye contact, practice it regularly.

- With experience, the fear of making eye contact will diminish, and you'll seamlessly maintain it while speaking.

Virtual Presentations:

- In virtual presentations, maintain eye contact by looking directly at the camera.

- Use a brightly colored sticker on your webcam as a visual cue to keep your focus on the camera.

- Position your webcam at eye level to achieve natural-looking eye contact.

Eye contact is a skill that improves with practice, and overcoming initial discomfort will lead to confident eye contact in both in-person and virtual presentations.

Be a tour guide with verbal pointing

A crucial aspect of successful technical presentations is guiding your audience through the visual content of your slides. When adopting a visual slide design, like the assertion evidence approach, your role is to narrate the slide's story. Imagine yourself as a tour guide for your slides, similar to a guide on a tour. A good guide helps you understand unfamiliar yet intriguing elements by pointing them out and explaining their significance. You should do the same through verbal pointing in your presentation.

Verbal pointing means aligning your words closely with what is on your slides, directing your audience's attention to specific elements and explaining their importance. By following these three steps — being descriptive, offering specific instructions, and explaining the significance — you can effectively engage your audience's attention during your presentation.

A blank screen is a power move

While striving for impeccable slides and flawless delivery, it is easy to become fixated on finding the perfect visual and crafting the perfect words. Yet, you might be surprised to discover that sometimes the most powerful action during a presentation is doing nothing. In other words, having a blank screen or no slides is a bold move that exudes confidence and allows the audience to concentrate solely on your spoken words.

Frequently, people ask, "What should I do when there's no visual for a topic I want to discuss?" The absence of a visual in such a situation is not a crisis. It simply means that a visual is not necessary at that point in your presentation. Remarkably, we've evolved to think that every presentation moment must involve a slide, but this is not the case. You, as the presenter, are the most critical aspect of the delivery. Show a slide only when it enhances your presentation. When no visual aids an idea, it signifies that you don't need a slide. This acknowledges the presenter's paramount importance.

There are likely several junctures in your presentation where the most impactful action you can take is to refrain from showing a slide and instead directly engage with the audience. This strategy can effectively alter the atmosphere in the room, surprising listeners and refocusing their attention on you. If you sense the audience's attention wandering, blanking the screen can be an effective way to regain their focus. Most remote slide advancers have a "blank screen" button, which you should familiarize yourself with. If you lack a remote control, you can use your keyboard by hitting "B" while in slideshow view to black out the screen, and press "B" again to undo it.

Consider employing a blank screen when conveying your most crucial information or significant recommendations. This approach displays your self-assuredness, allowing you to present the message entirely without relying on a slide and ensuring the audience is fully engaged with you. The use of a blank slide is an underutilized technique that can direct the audience's attention and underscore your confidence in your message.

A successful formula for transitions

A presentation consists of distinct components: the introduction (comprising a title and agenda slide), multiple middle slides, and a conclusion. Without deliberate planning, it is easy to transition from one piece or slide to another by simply stating, "And next, I will discuss," repeatedly. This approach can result in a jumble of information with no real cohesion.

To create a seamlessly flowing presentation like those given by admired speakers, it is crucial to establish connections among the components. Achieving this requires paying attention to the transitions between slides. When I mention transitions, I mean the spoken words that bridge the gap between slides. Verbal transitions add fluidity and elevate your presentation's quality. They establish links between different parts of your talk.

Thankfully, there is a formula for effective slide transitions every time. These transitions comprise both a summary and a preview. Start by summarizing the content of the current slide, followed by a preview of what is coming next. For example, "Now that we have seen the lower Q3 numbers than expected," (summary of the Q3 data), "we will proceed to explore two options for a stronger performance next quarter" (preview of the next topic). Employing this formula, you can create transitions on the fly as you progress between slides, without the need for memorization.

Transitions also benefit audience members who might have become distracted or needed to multitask briefly. When you provide a summary element, it serves as a final opportunity to ensure everyone has grasped the key points before moving on to the next topic. Consequently, there is no need to resort to dull phrases like, "On the next slide, I will talk about." Now, you can enhance the flow of your presentation by connecting slides with refined verbal transitions that summarize the previous content and preview the upcoming material. This technique will elevate your dynamic delivery.

Science not communicated is science not done

Scientific presentation skills will make your vital information more comprehensible, memorable, and actionable, significantly impacting both your work's progress and your career. Always remember, your role as a communicator is to bridge the gap between your technical expertise and your key stakeholders. Even the best idea holds little value if it is not understood or appreciated by others. Science without effective communication is incomplete. With your newfound skills, you are now equipped to effectively convey your scientific work to your audience.

Chapter 6 Establishing Credibility as a Speaker

Use your eyes

Imagine this: You are about to give a presentation. Before you utter a word, take a brief two-second pause and look at your audience. It's a simple yet powerful practice. However, some speakers rush through this crucial step, preoccupied with their notes or tech. But remember, your audience is the key to your presentation, and making eye contact signals respect and acknowledgment. This pause also conveys ease and confidence. For novice speakers, start by scanning your audience and find a friendly face to briefly acknowledge with a smile. Then, remember to connect with different audience members. To maintain strong eye contact throughout your presentation, divide the room into four quadrants and rotate through them, spending about two seconds with each person. For experienced speakers, consider the power move of making initial eye contact with someone neutral or even seemingly hostile. Smile if they meet your gaze. Winning them over early can boost your confidence. If not, simply shift your focus to another person. You are speaking to people, so look at them to engage your entire audience. This brief pause can make a big impact.

Look the part

Whether we admit it or not, we often judge people based on their clothing. To establish credibility, you should dress appropriately for your audience. If it is a business setting, consider wearing what your audience does or something slightly more formal. For example, if the audience is in business casual attire, you can wear business casual or even business formal. If you are uncertain about the dress code, contact the event organizer for guidance. They want you to look good because it reflects on them. There is one key exception to this rule: if you have a uniform or costume that signifies your authority, consider wearing it. For example, doctors can wear their white coats, police officers their uniforms, and astronauts their spacesuits when speaking about their respective fields. If you are an artist or a creative person, your unique style can be your uniform. Tech experts can embrace the latest tech fashion trends. Dressing in a way that aligns with your expertise can boost your credibility with the audience. Think about how your clothing choices can impact your credibility as you face your audience.

Consider your voice

When introducing yourself to your audience, focus on these three voice tips. First, be mindful of factors affecting volume. Maintain good posture, whether standing or sitting, and ensure you are facing your audience for better projection. If using a microphone, confirm that your levels are set correctly. Second, breathe naturally to avoid tense, shallow breaths. If you notice your shoulders rising, pause, take a normal breath, and continue. This helps you sound more composed. Third, warm up your voice before speaking. Practice saying your name deliberately by slowing down, pausing briefly between your first and last name, and perhaps over-enunciating if it is complex. Recording your name in a voicemail message and seeking feedback from colleagues can provide valuable insights into your pronunciation, pacing, and tone.

Read the room

"Reading the room" is the ability to understand and respond to the emotional state of your audience. To practice this skill, consider five key cues:

1. Context: Understand the purpose of the gathering, whether it is a casual event or a serious meeting.

2. Current Events: Be aware of any recent news that might influence your audience's mood.

3. Time of Day: Recognize how the time of day can affect energy levels and engagement.

4. Physical Environment: Assess the room size, formality, temperature, and other factors that could influence comfort.

5. Body Language: Observe obvious emotional cues from the audience's body language, such as smiles, frowns, or restlessness.

For example, if you are leading a half-day workshop in a new location and notice high humidity in the local headlines, see your audience dressed for warm weather, and feel the room is too cold, you might adjust your opening remarks to acknowledge the discomfort. If people are fidgeting after drinking coffee, you could consider incorporating an interactive task. The goal is to show empathy, address concerns, and build trust with your audience by adapting to their needs.

Use your body language and tone of voice

When starting a presentation, do not waste time telling your audience how you feel, like saying, "I am happy to be here." Instead, focus on understanding your audience's emotions. During a brief pause to observe your audience, consider their mood. If they seem happy or excited, it is great. You can feed off their energy. However, rather than stating your feelings, let your non-verbal cues do the talking. Smile genuinely and use a warm, sincere, and confident tone of voice to convey your emotions. Your audience is more likely to believe your authentic non-verbal communication than your words. So, show, do not tell, how you feel.

Deal with difficult audience emotions

When addressing an audience with mixed emotions, it is crucial to provide emotional leadership. You are like a guide leading them on a journey. Identify the most positive emotion in the room, often curiosity, and reflect it back to your audience. Use open-ended rhetorical questions to engage them. Your goal is to win over the curious individuals and gradually influence the rest. Even when faced with a seemingly entirely negative audience, reframe emotions positively. For example, boredom can be viewed as calm, and anger as concern. Show emotional leadership by respecting and elevating the positive aspects of their emotions to earn their attention and interest.

Research your audience

When addressing different audiences, it is essential to customize your opening remarks to their specific needs. Prior to your speech, thoroughly understand your audience by asking open-ended questions. Start with a general question like, "Tell me everything about the audience." Then explore into five key areas:

1. Gather demographic information, including gender, age, marital status, income, education, etc.

2. Discover their business details, such as the industries they represent, their job levels (students, interns, executives), and the companies they work for.

3. Assess their existing knowledge and concerns about your topic to tailor your content accordingly.

4. Determine their emotional stance toward your topic (enthusiastic, skeptical, etc.) to adjust your content's tone.

5. Seek any unique information about the audience that can help you establish credibility.

If possible, conduct independent research by obtaining a participant list and exploring their backgrounds through online profiles. Analyze both commonalities and distinctions among your audience members. This preparation will enable you to deliver a more tailored and effective presentation.

State your credentials

To establish your own credibility before a speech without sounding like you are bragging, follow these steps:

1. Create three columns on paper or your computer: Achievements, Education, and Experience.

2. Under "Achievements," list any external authority signifying your expertise, such as work titles, awards, companies, websites, books, or client testimonials.

3. In the "Education" column, note your degrees, coursework, and educational background.

4. In the "Experience" column, record the most relevant experiences to your topic and audience.

5. Choose one to three facts from these lists.

6. Use these facts to compose a brief self-introduction of 50 words or less. Focus on recent, relevant, and externally authoritative aspects.

7. Keep your introduction concise, relevant, and tailored to your audience and topic to maintain credibility without appearing arrogant.

Prepare for surprises

Earning credibility during a live presentation involves being prepared for unexpected situations. Explore three common scenarios to understand why preparation is crucial:

1. Host Absence: If the host, who was supposed to introduce you, does not show up, always be ready to introduce yourself. Do not solely rely on others to do the introduction.

2. Overlapping Content: If a previous speaker shares your planned opening story, quickly adapt by having an alternate and unique opening ready to maintain credibility.

3. Tech Failures: Technical issues can happen. Have a backup plan and consider how to engage the audience if technology completely fails. Be prepared to improvise and adapt to unexpected situations, demonstrating your ability to keep your cool and maintain credibility.

Prepare for these scenarios to smoothly handle surprises and maintain your credibility during live presentations.

Small room credibility: Case study

Examine a case study on building credibility in a small room. Tiffany is scheduled to present to a group of tech professionals at a company lunch and learn, but her host, Kevin, could not introduce her. Tiffany enters the chaotic room filled with casually dressed people, and she realizes her lunch plans with the group have changed due to the empty pizza boxes.

Tiffany's approach is commendable. She reads the room, observing the lively atmosphere, and decides not to mention the lunch situation to avoid embarrassment. Instead, she engages a curious individual in conversation, saying, "Well, I guess I better be super interesting because it looks like my talk is going to compete with your post-lunch pizza." After some laughter, she introduces herself, explains her role as a tech blogger, and seamlessly transitions into her presentation.

Tiffany adeptly establishes her credibility in the room. By making eye contact, engaging with an audience member, and mirroring the room's playful mood, she swiftly transforms from a stranger to a credible and engaging presenter in less than a minute.

Large room credibility: Case study

Analyze how a man named Thomas builds credibility in a large room during the first 30 seconds of his speech. Thomas is set to deliver a 20-minute presentation at a major all-day conference. Unfortunately, the person who was supposed to introduce him cannot make it, and Thomas is the first speaker at 8 AM. His audience primarily comprises middle-aged energy industry professionals in formal business attire, known for their conservative disposition. Thomas, having conducted audience research and scanned the latest news headlines about energy prices, walks into the room, which is unusually quiet.

Thomas notices the audience's curiosity as he stands before them in a hoodie and jeans, quite distinct from their business attire. To grab their attention, he opens by saying, "My name is Thomas Last year, I started a blog called Tech Talk with Thomas. Today, that blog has enjoyed over one million views. Now, you may be asking yourself, 'What does a tech blog written by one guy in a hoodie have to do with the energy industry?' In the next 20 minutes, I'm going to tell you three things I learned in my first year of blogging. I think you'll be able to apply these principles to your own line of work."

Thomas's approach is masterful; he adjusts his opening to align with the audience's curiosity and interests. He matches the subdued mood in the room initially but skillfully transitions to a tone of curiosity. His choice of words connects his credentials with the audience's concerns. While his attire, a hoodie and jeans, diverges from the typical business suits in the room, he chose this unconventional attire to reinforce his identity as a tech blogger.

Thomas's strategy shows his confidence in his content and presentation, taking a calculated wardrobe risk to stand out and be more memorable. He refrains from entering with excessive energy, instead opting for a calm and confident demeanor, catering to the audience's early morning disposition. Thomas earns high marks for establishing his credibility as a speaker.

Next steps

Start by practicing with a friendly audience and select low-risk events that would not have a significant impact on your career. Experiment with different opening approaches to connect with various audience moods, learning from both your successes and areas for improvement. Keep in mind that perfection is not necessary; every presentation is an emotional journey with opportunities for learning and growth. Positive changes may be gradual, so tracking your growth is essential.

Chapter 7 Presenting to Senior Executives

Understanding the executive audience

A high-level engineer seeking a senior government official's attention had just 45 seconds. Instead of a detailed presentation, he showed a single schematic of the state's bridge infrastructure, highlighting key points succinctly. To effectively communicate with time-crunched C-level executives, understand their need for brevity. Use a catchy one-sentence summary that piques their interest. Focus on the big picture, considering company history and industry trends. Support your message with essential facts and statistics, as executives make decisions based on evidence. Tailor your message to what matters most to the C-suite for maximum impact.

Communicating with senior executives before your presentation

To ensure a successful presentation to the executive team, your pre-meeting communication is crucial. Make sure the executive knows why you are there and what you need from them beforehand. Here are key components for effective pre-meeting messaging:

1. Do your homework: Gather essential information about the executive, such as their planning timeline, preferred communication method, and any pre-read preferences.

2. Pick your champions: Having someone who can vouch for you and your content can build credibility.

3. Share the hook, what, why plan: Include the message headline, a brief content preview, and why the information is relevant in your pre-meeting communication.

4. Set expectations: Clearly communicate the purpose of the meeting and what you expect from the executives (discussion, decision, approval, etc.) in your pre-meeting email.

Before your meeting, consider sharing the necessary information and expectations to set the stage for success.

Anticipating tough questions from senior executives

When presenting to the C-suite, you will face unique challenges. They may interrupt you within seconds, so it is crucial to avoid common rookie mistakes. Here are the key points to remember:

1. Never tell them to wait when interrupted; be prepared for continuous interruptions.

2. Avoid a linear game plan; anticipate possible questions and incorporate additional data in your presentation.

3. Engage in a conversational tone during Q&A, providing more context and rationale in your responses.

4. To sound more natural, use "magical words" like "imagine this" or "for example" to connect concepts to real-life examples and applications.

Remember that the Q&A session is as vital as your presentation, so allocate a significant portion of your preparation to address questions from executives effectively.

Framing your message to senior executives

Just like a captivating movie trailer, the opening lines of your presentation are crucial to grab your executive audience's attention and set up their expectations. Whether your message is informative or persuasive, your framing matters. For informative messages, start with a brief executive summary of key points and their relevance. In persuasive messages, begin with a problem or opportunity, followed by your solution and supporting evidence.

Example 1 (Informative): Maria shares top research findings with her marketing firm executives, creating interest and curiosity with succinct points.

Example 2 (Persuasive): If Maria were pitching a new marketing strategy, she would use a story to highlight the problem, propose a solution, and provide supporting statistics.

In both cases, focus on engaging emotions initially, followed by a strong presentation of facts and logic. Practice and a confident delivery are essential for capturing your audience's attention.

Make your presentation valuable for senior executives

To create value in a presentation to senior executives, go beyond their initial request by understanding their informational needs and delivering accordingly. Your message's core should rely on evidence-based logic, such as return on investment calculations or statistics guiding informed decisions. Different types of evidence to strengthen your message include:

1. Facts: Include relevant, essential facts in your presentation, contextualized for maximum impact, such as recent sales data or customer satisfaction rates.

2. Statistics: Use statistics from credible sources, whether external reports or proprietary research, to help the audience understand issues and answer questions.

3. Testimonials: Incorporate customer or client testimonials to add a personal dimension to your numerical data, making it more relatable.

4. Examples: Share context-specific examples that bring your information to life and engage the audience.

5. Calculations: Be prepared to present various business calculations like break-even analysis, net present value, return on investment, or conversion ratios, depending on your audience's language.

Ensure your sources are credible and context-specific. Tailor your evidence to align with your organization's logic, creating value in your message for senior executives.

Engage your executive audience with relevant stories

To engage your audience effectively in a presentation, ensure that your message introduction is captivating, like a movie trailer, and provides a substantial and memorable storyline or theme. Use standard story design principles with a "once upon a time" setup, progression with phrases like "and then one day" or "because of that," and a resolution that unveils your proposed solution.

Here are three additional strategies for emotional appeal:

1. Create a powerful narrative: Craft your message in a story format, using relatable characters and situations. Connect your points back to the story throughout the presentation.

2. Be one with your audience: Use language, phrases, and references that are important to your executives. Align your idea with strategic initiatives or leadership priorities to show your contribution to the company's greater good.

3. Use visual and detailed language: Employ visual words and powerful phrases that evoke emotion. Describe situations vividly to engage your audience's feelings.

Develop a memorable story flow for your presentation.

Following up with senior executives

To ensure your post-meeting communication is effective, timely, and appreciated by the executive team, follow these key steps:

1. Timing is critical. Send your follow-up note promptly, especially if the meeting was at the end of the day, to keep the discussions fresh in their minds.

2. Express appreciation for their time sincerely but not meekly, acknowledging their contribution to fruitful discussions that moved issues forward.

3. Summarize the meeting content, highlighting main topics and decisions made, and include details about follow-up activities for reference in the future.

4. Follow up on action items, showing progress and providing a clear description of goals and expected completion dates.

5. Include key data and relevant resources in the document, and invite questions and follow-up.

A well-crafted follow-up note, like the one Maria sent to marketing executives, summarizes the discussion, decisions, and next steps, demonstrating ownership and initiative. Prepare your follow-up note in advance for your next high-visibility project meeting with the executive team.

Navigating last minute meeting time crunches

To develop the essential skill of presentation flexibility for dealing with unexpected time constraints, follow these strategies:

1. Have a general summary slide: Prepare a key content slide that serves as a quick summary of your presentation, which you can use when time is limited.

2. Develop a tagline: Create a strong tagline that expresses the "what," "why," and "how" of your idea, enabling you to deliver a concise pitch when needed.

3. Cut to 10%: Design your presentation as usual and then cut all but the essential 10% of content to reveal the core of your message when time is restricted.

4. Load the Q&A: Allocate a substantial portion of your allotted time for discussion and questions, allowing for a more engaging interaction with the audience.

By being prepared and nimble in handling time constraints, you can make a positive impression when presenting to senior executives.

Redirecting a distracted audience

Distractions in front of an executive audience can disrupt your presentation. Here are ways to address common distractions:

1. Technology Distractions: If executives are focused on their phones or email, engage directly with your slides, emphasize key points, and alter your intonation to regain their attention. Know your audience's behavior to stay prepared.

2. Side Conversations: If a side conversation arises, pause and diplomatically ask if you should proceed or if it's a good time for discussion. If it turns into an argument, redirect to the main theme or let them decide the course of action.

3. Personal Agenda: When an executive pushes their own idea or repeatedly interrupts, acknowledge their input and gently steer the discussion back to the meeting's goals. Consider seeking allies within the group to assist in redirecting.

Distracted executive audiences are common, and while it may be challenging to regain their attention, you can prepare for and effectively manage these distractions to convey your message.

Managing interruptions while presenting

To succeed in presenting to executives, you must remain flexible when dealing with interruptions. Your ability to manage interruptions while maintaining warmth and competence can enhance your credibility.

1. Exuding Warmth During Interruptions:

   - Listen attentively, focusing on non-verbal cues like nodding, making eye contact, and acknowledging the interruption.

   - Quickly assess whether the interruption is a question or comment. Respond with rapport-building phrases that connect with the executive.

   - When answering direct questions, provide evaluative responses rather than simple yes or no answers.

   - If the interruption isn't a question or comment but a distraction, decide whether to continue or pause, demonstrating professionalism.

2. Exuding Competence During Interruptions:

   - Your responses depend on your preparedness. Practice your content in sections, allowing for easy pivoting.

   - Be ready to go deeper into your content if needed. Have hyperlinked slides or appendix pages to access additional information.

   - Prezi, a presentation tool using drill-down animation, can serve as an analogy. The main idea fits on one slide, with branches for detailed information.

Interruptions can be an opportunity to display your readiness and establish trust with your audience.

Practicing for high-stakes presentations

Exposure to top-level executives can significantly boost your career. The design a logical and narrative-driven message that adds value for executive audiences. When following up, focus on actionable and relationship-building communication. The path to presenting to the C-suite is a long-term plan. Begin by participating more in meetings and volunteering for cross-department projects to increase your visibility within the company. Practicing and excelling in these skills will bring you closer to your goal.

Chapter 8 Executive Presence on Video Conference Calls

Expectations and preparation

If you prepare and dress appropriately for an in-person meeting, the same level of effort should be put into your video meetings. Remember, it might be the first-time others see you, making first impressions crucial. Before diving into video meeting preparation, let is address what to expect during a video call.

Recognize that video communication may feel different and somewhat awkward as you're speaking to a camera instead of people. In group video conferencing, there might be silences or people talking over each other, which is normal. Understanding these dynamics beforehand reduces surprises.

Explore different scenarios you might encounter in video meetings:

1. Giving a presentation to a remote audience: If you are presenting a PowerPoint, viewers will likely see it in full screen. Keep the presentation high-level with minimal text and incorporate visuals that support your points to ensure it is engaging. Avoid making it dense or distracting, as it will be the primary focus while you speak.

2. Leading a live discussion with remote team members: Prepare an agenda in advance to maintain an organized flow. Since everyone is not in the same room, an agenda helps keep the discussion productive and on track, demonstrating your readiness and leadership.

3. Conducting a one-on-one video meeting: Have all necessary materials in front of you, preferably printed or written out. Avoid toggling between screens during the meeting. Maintain eye contact with the camera as a sign of respect, just as you would in an in-person conversation.

Introducing yourself and speaking up

Introducing yourself and speaking up in a video meeting presents some unique challenges, but there are effective ways to navigate this situation. Here are key points to consider:

1. If you are leading the video meeting, encourage participants to introduce themselves when they speak. This demonstrates leadership and helps everyone associate names with faces in a remote setting.

2. Even if you are not leading the meeting, take the initiative to introduce yourself before speaking. This not only piques listeners' interest but also conveys confidence and authority, making your points more impactful.

3. Choose the right moment to speak, ideally during a brief pause or when someone is concluding their point. Avoid interrupting others, as it can come across as rude and disrupt the professional atmosphere.

4. Use the instant messaging function in video conferencing software to post a pending question if necessary. This can prompt someone to address it or indicate to others that it is an unresolved issue.

5. Address individuals directly by using their names when speaking to them on video. Since traditional body language cues are limited in a video conference, using names ensures clear communication and engagement.

Incorporate these strategies in your next video meeting to establish your presence effectively, as even small actions can leave a significant impact.

Keeping it engaging

Video conferences can be prone to distractions and may lack the typical in-person cues, but as an executive, you can make them engaging and effective.

1. Stay attentive and perceptive to encourage active participation from everyone. Since participants are in different locations, watch their reactions on the screen and listen to their input to gauge the dynamics.

2. Take the lead in guiding the conversation. If it veers off-topic, use your authority to steer it back in the right direction, as you don't have the physical presence to provide cues.

3. Address debates or conflicts by speaking up and calming the situation. You can even use hand signals, which you should inform participants about before

the meeting, to indicate when they should stop talking, particularly when it gets chaotic.

4. When engagement lags, take the initiative to transition topics and ask questions to stimulate discussion. Direct questions at qualified individuals who may be hesitant to speak in a video conference setting.

5. Conclude the conference by inviting questions, ensuring that everyone has an opportunity to voice their opinions, even in a remote setting.

Being an effective leader in a video conference requires awareness and active involvement, even when physical proximity is absent.

Using visuals to support your content

Great meetings and presentations often stand out due to an element of surprise, whether it is offering new insights or presenting unexpectedly interesting visuals. In video meetings, you have a unique chance to make a lasting impression on remote viewers, so consider them as vital as in-person meetings.

When leading a video meeting, boost your executive presence by creatively showcasing your key points and enhancing takeaways. PowerPoint presentations are effective for visual communication. If you are not using PowerPoint, utilize screen-sharing features available on many video platforms to display images or videos. Additionally, if the discussion revolves around a product, having it on hand to display during the meeting demonstrates preparation and proactivity.

Even if you are not leading the meeting, preparing visuals to support your points can demonstrate your proactive involvement and enhance your credibility with the audience.

Enhancing your conversations

Half of what contributes to a great video presentation involves planning your content, but the other half relates to anticipating and addressing potential distractions that could disrupt your meeting. To ensure the most effective presentation, consider the following steps:

1. Mute your microphone when you are not speaking to prevent the transmission of outside noises or distractions like music or background chatter. Unmute when you need to participate.

2. Set your phone to silent mode before the video meeting to prevent interruptions like incoming calls or message notifications. This minimizes distractions and maintains your focus.

3. If feasible, choose a quiet room and close the door to create a distraction-free environment, even if your microphone is muted.

4. Avoid checking your emails or browsing the web during the video conference. This is similar to maintaining eye contact and attention in an in-person conversation and is important for conveying respect and attentiveness.

By adhering to these four simple rules, you can ensure that your presentation is as effective as possible.

Perfecting eye contact

Maintaining good eye contact in a video conference is crucial, as it significantly enhances your presence. The key is to adapt your eye contact based on the type of video meeting you are in.

1. For informal video meetings where it is a group discussion with equal participation, looking at the screen is natural and acceptable. You'll need to see others and read their body language on the screen, so looking at the screen while speaking is the right approach in this scenario.

2. In formal video presentations where you are the main speaker, ensure you maintain eye contact with the camera lens. This is because all eyes are on you, and looking directly into the camera gives the impression that you're engaging with your audience. It enhances your presence and authority.

Consider the difference in your appearance when you switch your eye contact between the screen and the camera lens. By understanding the meeting scenario and adjusting your eye contact accordingly, you can make a significant impact on your video presence.

Hand gestures on video

Our hands are a powerful tool to emphasize key points during a presentation, but they must be used thoughtfully in a video setting. Even though you might be in a remote location, it is important to be aware that your hand movements are still visible to your audience.

1. Use hand gestures to emphasize the significance of a statement, pushing your point forward.

2. Employ hand gestures to illustrate numbers or quantify and qualify your ideas. For instance, you can show "three" proposals with your fingers or indicate the size of an idea.

3. These movements can enhance your on-camera presentation skills when all eyes are on you.

However, improper hand usage can be distracting. Avoid frantic waving or aggressive pointing at the camera. Additionally, when you are not speaking and listening, refrain from folding your arms, as it may convey disengagement. Always remember that others on the video call can see your actions, so use your hands to support your message rather than hinder it.

Using confident body posture

During a video call, your body posture plays a crucial role in conveying confidence and engagement, whether you are speaking or listening.

1. Maintain an appropriate distance between you and the camera when sitting.

2. If you are speaking or presenting, sit on the front half of your chair, not all the way back, as this posture is used by TV news anchors to project their voices.

3. Keep your back straight, lean slightly forward, and relax your shoulders to appear engaged and professional.

4. When speaking, maintain eye contact by looking directly at the camera lens, creating a connection with the viewer.

5. Avoid slouching or sitting too far back, as it may give the impression of carelessness during presentations.

On the other hand, if you are not presenting, you can be slightly more relaxed but should remain alert. Stay focused on the screen and be prepared to engage in the conversation by moving to the edge of your chair. Sitting with good posture not only affects how others perceive you but also helps ensure your voice is heard clearly.

Wardrobe choices

In video meetings, location does not matter, but your appearance, at least from the waist up, is crucial. Choose professional attire for the upper half, such as a blouse and blazer for women or a dress shirt and suit jacket for men. You can keep it casual from the waist down if the camera does not capture it.

When it comes to styling, opt for solid jewel-tone colors like sapphire blue, emerald green, turquoise, or ruby red. Brighter colors work well and add vibrancy. Avoid distracting patterns like florals or stripes, along with shiny fabrics like silk and satin, as they can reflect light. Also, steer clear of fussy details like frilly collars and excessive buttons that may divert attention when you speak. Your goal is to stand out for the right reasons.

Positioning your camera

Improving your video conferencing setup is vital for a better experience. Elevate your camera by placing your laptop on a book or a box to achieve an eye-level perspective, which not only looks more flattering but also promotes better posture. Before starting a video call, check your setup to ensure that your camera is appropriately positioned, minimizing the gap above your head and framing more of your upper body. A small camera angle adjustment can significantly impact how others perceive you, so always test your camera setup before meeting with others.

Lighting is the key

While your video conferencing may not align with the golden hour photographers adore, it is crucial to consider lighting for a flattering appearance. Here are tips for optimizing your home lighting:

1. Position your camera to face the light source. Natural light from a window is ideal, but avoid direct sunlight that creates harsh shadows.

2. If sunlight enters the room, partially lower the blinds to soften the light while retaining a pleasant glow.

3. Ensure the light source is never behind you, as it darkens your video and obscures your face. It is vital for proper visibility.

4. In windowless rooms or unfavorable lighting, place a lamp nearby to enhance your visibility.

Improving your lighting setup can significantly enhance your video quality and appearance.

Crisp and clear audio

Avoid awkward pauses and audio issues that disrupt your conversations and professionalism. Prepare to ensure crisp and clear audio:

1. Test your connection beforehand by calling someone and verifying audio quality.

2. Confirm your surroundings are quiet and free from distractions: turn off music, close unnecessary windows, and silence your phone.

3. In a noisy environment, use a headset with a built-in microphone, positioning it closer to your mouth for better clarity.

Spend 20 minutes before your meeting to address potential audio problems, guaranteeing a smooth and effective conversation.

Backdrops and backgrounds

While video conferencing from home offers convenience, it is crucial to consider your background. Keep your surroundings professional:

1. Ensure a clean and tidy environment free from distractions, like kids' toys or clutter.

2. If you have a home office, close the door to reduce noise and maintain privacy.

3. Consider using a backdrop or divider to hide personal items and minimize distractions during video meetings.

Maintain professionalism by focusing on your background, allowing the focus to be on you.

Tips to help you stand out

Enhance your leadership in video presentations with these pro tips:

1. Assign someone, like an assistant, to take notes during the call, creating a record of key points.

2. Provide a hard copy of the material for reference.

3. Announce the note-taking and sharing of notes at the beginning of the call to impress your audience.

4. Consider recording the presentation for those who cannot attend, ensuring a wider audience can benefit. Remember to inform participants of the recording.

These thoughtful steps can make a lasting impression during video meetings.

Practice run

After reviewing how to establish a professional presence in video conferences, here is your practice checklist:

1. Ensure your on-camera attire is professional and eliminate distracting elements from your environment.

2. Test your internet connection, audio setup, and camera positioning for the best appearance.

3. Close unnecessary software and set your phone to silent.

4. Verify everything by having a friend or colleague test your setup.

With these preparations, you can confidently shine in your upcoming meetings, leaving a lasting positive impression.

Chapter 9 Managing Your Anxiety While Presenting

Managing physical anxiety symptoms

Experiencing symptoms like a racing heart, sweaty palms, shaky legs, and a dry mouth before a presentation is common and natural. However, these symptoms can make you appear nervous and feel uncomfortable. To manage them and appear more confident to your audience, it is essential to embrace your anxiety. Acknowledge that it is normal and that you have the right to feel nervous when speaking in front of others. Greeting your anxiety in this way gives you space to address the symptoms effectively. Here are some techniques to manage specific symptoms:

1. For a racing heart, practice deep belly breaths to slow your heart rate.

2. Combat sweaty palms and dry mouth by using a lozenge, chewing gum, or drinking warm water.

3. Reduce perspiration by holding something cold in your palms.

4. If you are speaking quickly due to shallow breathing, take deep breaths to slow down. Broad gestures can also help pace your speech.

5. To prevent swaying, position your feet parallel under your shoulders, which stabilizes your hips and minimizes swaying tendencies.

By combining these symptom management strategies with acknowledging and accepting your anxiety, you can feel more comfortable and project confidence to your audience.

Managing mental anxiety symptoms

When experiencing anxiety related to public speaking, many people encounter mental symptoms like losing focus, fixating on a single idea, or the fear of forgetting their content. To address the common issue of blanking out during a speech, consider these techniques:

1. Instead of admitting you have blanked out, retrace your steps by restating what you have just said, helping you regain your place.

2. Prepare a "back pocket question" in advance that you can ask your audience if you forget your content. While they ponder their responses, you will have time to gather your thoughts.

3. Restating the purpose or goal of your presentation can help you recover if you blank out. A well-structured presentation should have a clear goal or purpose that you can revisit.

Using these techniques can assist you if you find yourself blanking out during a presentation, and knowing about them can actually reduce the likelihood of experiencing this issue in the first place.

Catastrophizing while speaking in public

Many people fear public speaking more than death itself, as humorously noted by Jerry Seinfeld. This fear can become highly emotional and irrational. To address this, try these rationalizing techniques:

1. Make a list of your public speaking fears and concerns.

2. Assign a likelihood percentage to each fear, acknowledging that these fears don't always materialize.

3. Consider the worst-case scenario if one of your fears were to come true. For example, if you blank out during a speech, it might be embarrassing, but it is a manageable situation.

By systematically rationalizing your fears, you regain a sense of control and can reduce anxiety associated with public speaking.

Being judged while speaking in public

When facing an audience, whether in person or virtually, the fear of judgment and evaluation can be overwhelming. To alleviate this anxiety, there are effective strategies:

1. Start your presentation with an attention-grabbing activity, such as a video, a poll, a question, or a compelling image. This shifts the audience's focus away from scrutinizing you, providing you with time to gather your thoughts.

2. Visualization can be powerful. Imagine yourself delivering your presentation or leading a meeting in your mind to desensitize yourself to the evaluation.

3. Utilize technology like the Virtual Speech app, which simulates speaking environments, audience sizes, and even audience attitudes. This helps you become accustomed to the judgment and evaluation you might face.

By combining these techniques and redirecting audience attention, you can increase your confidence and comfort when presenting, making you a more compelling speaker.

Future impact of speaking in public

When communicating, we often fear not achieving our goals, leading to speaking anxiety. To address this future fear, consider two approaches:

1. Contingency planning involves preparing for potential issues that make you nervous, like having backup systems or resources to handle unexpected problems.

2. Become present-oriented to focus on the moment, reducing concerns about the future. Techniques include engaging with your audience, listening to music, counting backward, or saying a tongue twister before presenting.

These strategies alleviate future fears, boost your confidence, and enhance your ability to connect with your audience.

Procrastination, perfectionism, PowerPoint

Many of us inadvertently worsen our speaking anxiety by engaging in certain behaviors I refer to as the "three Ps."

1. Procrastination: Delaying preparation exacerbates anxiety as the communication date approaches. Combat procrastination by publicly committing to a schedule and rewarding yourself for each completed step.

2. Perfectionism: Striving for perfection in communication is counterproductive. Shift your focus from achieving perfection to being audience-centric. This change not only reduces the need for perfection but also enhances audience engagement.

3. PowerPoint: Overemphasizing slides in presentations can hinder your confidence. Prioritize your story and message before considering whether slides would enhance your communication. By putting your story first and slides second, you'll equip yourself to present confidently and effectively.

Addressing these three Ps—procrastination, perfectionism, and PowerPoint— can boost your confidence, lessen anxiety, and improve your overall communication skills.

Do not memorize

Many anxious speakers opt for memorization, thinking it will reduce anxiety, but this approach has the opposite effect. Memorizing increases pressure to recite exact wording and hinders engagement with the audience. Instead, consider using an outline for your presentation.

You can start with a full manuscript if needed, especially for new or non-native language content. Then, create an outline – either a bulleted list of key points or a question-based outline focused on addressing unasked questions from your audience. Practice from your outline, breaking your sessions into manageable chunks. It is beneficial to record yourself speaking the presentation and review it, focusing separately on content and non-verbal delivery. This approach builds confidence without the need for strict memorization.

How do I live my anxiety plan?

Lao Tzu once said, "The journey of a thousand miles begins with a single step." This rings true for addressing speaking anxiety. To manage anxiety, consider creating an Anxiety Management Plan (AMP) – a personalized acronym or mantra. Each person's AMP is unique, but here's an example using "BRAVE":

- Breathe: Take deep breaths before starting.

- Rationalize: Evaluate your fears and their rationality.

- Audience-Focused: Shift focus from yourself to your audience.

- Visualize: Envision success before speaking.

- Enjoy and Engage: Be present in the moment, avoiding worry about the future.

By embracing an AMP, you can boost your confidence, connect with your audience, and become a more courageous presenter, whether you are speaking at a meeting, wedding, pitch, or any other situation.